ROLLER COASTER

David Bennett

ROLLER COASTER

WOODEN AND STEEL COASTERS, TWISTERS AND CORKSCREWS

CHARTWELL
BOOKS, INC.

A QUINTET BOOK

Published by **Chartwell Books**

A Division of **Book Sales, Inc.**

114, Northfield Avenue

Edison, New Jersey 08837

ISBN 0-7858-0885-X

This book was designed and produced by

Quintet Publishing Limited

6 Blundell Street

London N7 9BH

Creative Director: Richard Dewing

Art Director: Clare Reynolds

Designer: Andrea Bettella

Senior Editor: Sally Green

Editor: Rosie Hankin

Illustrator: Julian Baker

Typeset in Great Britain by

Central Southern Typesetters, Eastbourne

Manufactured in Singapore by Universal Graphics Pte Ltd

Printed in China by Leefung-Asco Printers Ltd

CONTENTS

FOREWORD

▲ Ride ticket for the famous Bobs at Riverview Park, Chicago.

▶ Kumba coaster, Busch Gardens, Tampa, Florida.

The origins of the roller coaster will probably never be a settled issue, historians and coaster enthusiasts could argue the case for any one of three contentious claims with equal conviction. Was it a distant second cousin of the elaborate ice slides of St. Petersburg in sixteenth-century Russia, or a half-brother to the magnificent wooden toboggan rides which were fashionable in Paris a century later, or a direct descendent of the gravity rail road in the Mauch Chunk Valley in Pennsylvania in 1827?

In a way this excuse for debate and discussion as to who was first parodies the competitive, commercial world of tourism and leisure industry over the past century and the colorful history of the roller coaster. The success and evolution of the roller coaster and white knuckle ride has inextricably mirrored the growth and changing perception of the amusement park industry over the years.

Not all of it has been a smooth ride for the roller coaster industry. Economic boom has been followed with monotonous regularity by catastrophic failure and collapse, brought about by war, economic depression, or the whims of fashion. Periods of intense innovation and development in roller coaster science have been interrupted by long periods of decline and neglect. But with each era of success, something new and breathtaking in ride intensity has emerged. We are currently enjoying a long period of economic stability and as a result we are witnessing an amazing growth in roller coaster production, with 100 m.p.h. rides now under construction, as roller coasters set the fashion for thrill rides again at the end of the century.

Who were the great pioneers of the roller coaster? Which ride was the most terrifying in the world? Can a roller coaster accelerate faster than a racing car and deliver as much g force as a fighter aircraft? What is the difference between a steel and wooden roller coaster, and a heart line spin and free fall ride? How does the g force work on the body during the ride? How safe is it to ride a roller coaster? Which amusement parks have the top roller coaster rides? What is a chain dog? By the end of this book I hope you will get an explanation and answer to all these questions and a fascinating insight into the world of the roller coaster. Who knows you may even want to join an enthusiasts club or visit a particular park on your vacation to compare the ride intensity of say a John Miller coaster with a Curtis Summers design. Now that would be something. It's like comparing a Bentley with a Cadillac.

I am indebted to Barry Norman for his considerable help with sourcing archive material and proof-reading, to Justin Garvanovic for copies of *First Drop* magazine, and to my partner Jenny Crossley for living through the chaos while I wrote this book. I wish to acknowledge the reference books that I have used as my bibles of facts—Robert Cartmell's

Incredible Scream Machine (Amusement Park Books, Inc., 1987), Richard Munch's *Harry Traver: Legends Of Terror* (Amusement Park Books, Inc., 1982), and Judith Adams' *The American Amusement Park Industry* (Twayne Publishers, Boston, USA, 1991).

▲ The magnificent Promenades Aeriennes built in the
Beaujon Gardens, Paris, in 1817, was one of the
earliest wheeled toboggan rides on a wooden track.

CHAPTER ONE

ORIGINS OF THE ROLLER COASTER

RUSSIAN ICE SLIDES

Imagine it has been snowing for a month, the landscape is ice blue, the ponds and rivers are frozen hard. You and your guests are getting bored stuck inside day after day as the ice and snow crystallize deeper on the horizon. All horse riding has been cancelled and there are no game birds to shoot at, but someone has suggested the bright idea of sliding down the slopes of ice and snow on the high ground of the estate. It sounds great fun and just the thing to break the boredom of winter. So the nobleman, courtiers, gentry, and townsfolk of St. Petersburg took to the slopes in the snow and before long ice slides had become a national pastime for the whole country.

Could a popular winter sport in fifteenth-century Russia suggest the beginnings of the roller coaster? By the turn of the sixteenth century, the Russian ice slides had become marvels of wooden construction, skillfully crafted and handsomely decorated, some flanked by rows of fir trees to enclose the ride, some built with a drop of 70 feet and a slope angled at 50 degrees. That's about as steep as the first drop of some of the fastest roller coasters in the late 1920s! An ice block was used as a sled, with the top hollowed out and lined with wood and wool for the rider to sit on. There was a short rope tied through a hole in the ice block to guide the sled down the ice-covered track. Daily watering of the wooden slope kept the ice smooth and fast. The rides became so popular that they were even built indoors on waxed wooden slopes and used at night by lighting up the runs with torches.

The first crude roller coaster was a Russian invention, although it was strictly not a wheeled ride. So where was the first true wheeled coaster ride developed? It is alleged that during the Napoleonic Wars, returning French soldiers, having spent many months enduring a typical Russian winter and no doubt enjoying Russian ice slides, introduced the idea into French society. But instead of building ice slopes, French entrepreneurs built dry slides probably because the French winter was a short season and it made commercial sense to stretch the season into summer. Sitting on small wheeled boards, the riders were hurtled dangerously along a wooden track that dipped up and down on the way to the bottom.

Such was the public interest in dry slides in Paris that in 1817 two magnificent wheeled roller coaster rides were opened, the Les Montagnes Russes at Belleville and the Promandes Aeriennes in the beautiful Beaujon Gardens in Paris. They contained many features that are seen on today's roller coasters. The wooden cars—which could reach speeds in excess of 30 m.p.h.—were locked to the tracks by the wheel axles projecting into grooves cut in the walls of the wooden guide rails. The ride itself consisted of two parallel but separate

▲ An example of a sixteenth-century Russian ice slide in St. Petersburg, built for the aristocracy and gentry, featuring a long down slope and highly decorative entry towers.

▼ Many wooden Russian Mountain-style dry slides such as this were built in lavish parks around Paris in the 1800s.

tracks with the wooden cars leaving in pairs from the top of the slope and circling to the left or right on reaching the bottom. Attendants would then push the cars back to the top. A primitive cable system invented in 1826 by M. Lebonjer was later added to haul the cars to the top. Many would argue that Paris was the birthplace of the first roller coaster.

Historian Robert Cartmell suggests that a wheel roller coaster, referred to as a Switchback, existed as early as 1784 in Russia. The ride was built in the Gardens of Oreinbaum in St. Petersburg and was part of a fantasy pleasure complex called Katalnaya Gorka. In winter the conventional ice sleds would operate, but in summer wheeled carriages were placed in grooved tracks to run down an undulating course, very like the early switchback coasters.

Russian ice slides, popularly known as "Russian Mountains" disappeared by the middle of the nineteenth century as public interest in the sport evaporated. Today, in Chapultepec Park, Mexico, is one of the great wooden roller coaster rides, "La Montana Rusa," named after the early Russian slides, and acknowledging the historical precedent. But are Russian ice slides and wooden switchbacks the forerunners of the modern roller coaster, or is it the gravity railroad in the Mauch Valley in the U.S., or the pioneering rides of La Marcus Adna Thompson?

THE MAUCH CHUNK RAILROAD

The idea of using gravity to run a railroad was exploited cleverly by a mining company in Pennsylvania in 1827. The railroad was built by Josiah White and Erskine Hazard to haul coal from strip mines high up in Summit Hill down to the Lehigh Canal in Mauch Chunk, some 18 miles away.

With the slope from Summit Hill to Mauch Chunk dropping 96 feet every mile, the train needed only a gentle nudge to speed it on its way down the mountain. A single track was made along the lush green mountainside and wooden rails were laid, topped with flat iron running plate imported from England. Loaded coal wagons were connected in trains of six to fourteen cars depending on the quantity of coal mined that day. A brake man, or runner as they were called, sat at the back of the last wagon gripping on to an upright brake as the train accelerated down the track.

The trip down the valley took a half-hour, but the uphill return leg was an ordeal for the mules that hauled the wagons back, taking three hours. By 1844, as the railroad network expanded in the U.S. and coal became the major fuel source for industry, a faster and more economical method for transporting coal down from Summit Hill was needed. The single track was proving to be a bottleneck. So Josiah White set about building a second track to haul empty trains back up to Summit Hill, forming a figure-eight track that permitted a continuous flow of trains up and down the mountainside. Two huge stationary steam engines, each generating 120 horsepower, were installed to haul the cars uphill. One was positioned at the top of Mount Pisgah and the other on Mount

▲ Looking up Mt. Pisgah Plane on the Mauch Chunk Gravity Railroad, Pennsylvania, which started a fare-paying passenger service in 1872. The "barney" is being coupled to the car, to push it up the incline.

▲ Midway up Mt. Pisgah Plane, the first of two inclines to Summit Hill, with the "barney" in the rear.

◄ Later wheeled toboggan rides such as this one built at Innenburener, Germany, ran on rails built into the wooden track.

▲ "The Crossover," with the car bridging the down track, as it ascends the second incline up Mt. Jefferson Plane

Jefferson six miles away. A small flat four-wheeled car called a "barney" linked by cable to the engines, pushed the cars up the steep incline to the top of each hill. At the top of the hill, the cars rolled down the slope by gravity to the bottom of the next hill, where another "barney" then attached itself to the train and pushed it to the top. A series of antiroll back ratchets was also attached to the inclined track. It was a safety feature that was to become an integral part of all modern roller coaster rides. At Mount Jefferson the new track was linked to the original gravity rail. It was here that trains were loaded and then coasted down 18 miles of scenic countryside en route to Mauch Chunk.

Sadly by the time the new route was in place and operating successfully, the Mauch Chunk railroad was to become obsolete. In February 1872, the Hauto Rail Tunnel was completed through nearby North Mountain bringing the national railways directly to the mine. The figure-eight track stretching a total of 18 miles was turned into a tourist attraction, with trainloads of people soon coming from all over the country to ride this engineering wonder. By 1874 the Mauch Chunk Scenic Railroad was the second largest tourist attraction in the U.S. after Niagara Falls, with over 35,000 visitors enjoying the panoramic views of the Blue Ridge Mountains and the Lehigh Valley.

The cost of the trip was one dollar with the round trip up to Summit Hill taking one hour and twenty minutes. At the top there was an hotel, the Switchback restaurant, guided walking tours of the area, and a chance to see the "Amazing Burning Mines" of sulfur which burned continuously. After the walking tours and a rest, passengers reboarded the train to begin the gravity ride down to Mauch Chunk. Most of them were not prepared for what they were about to experience. Here is a description taken from a report in the *Valley Gazette* of Lansford:

"... the car spun along at frightening speed. On a curve a man's straw hat flew into the air like a kite. Women dug their nails into the wooden seats to keep them from being whisked out of the car... A little boy lost the button on his shirt. His mother's grip on him was like a vice. He wondered why she looked so pale. The ladies were struggling to keep their skirts down over their knees, but the driver showed no mercy. Faster they went until birches, pines, hemlocks, rocks, stumps, earth, and sky all blurred into one. Plunging down the hill they could hardly remain seated. Rounding corners, everyone was flying to the opposite side in a squeezing

▲ The route of the figure-eight round trip, of the Mauch Chunk Gravity Railroad, starting from the Lehigh River. All but one mile of the 18-mile journey was by gravity. This print was taken from an original tourist leaflet.

La Marcus Thompson's first switchback roller coaster opened on June 13, 1884, at Coney Island, Brooklyn, New York.

heap. The elderly man whose straw hat vanished began to wonder why he came. His will wasn't in order and the valley looked like it was a hundred miles straight down. The small boy was beginning to enjoy the ride, but his mother felt she was going to faint."

The Mauch Chunk was unquestionably the first mechanical roller coaster ride in the U.S. and one of the very first railroads to be built. Its influence on roller coaster design and development in the years that followed was inestimable. It still holds the record for the highest altitude (1,260 feet) and longest length (18 miles) of track ever built.

The Mauch Chunk Switchback was declared an historical monument in 1976. Tracks can still be found along the old route but all other traces have disappeared. There is talk of rebuilding and restoring the Switchback one day.

LA MARCUS ADNA THOMPSON

La Marcus Adna Thompson was born on March 8, 1848, in Jersey, Ohio, and was the eighth of ten children born to his farming parents. His inventive mind was soon evident when at the age of twelve he devised a butter churn for his mother, had invented a miniature sawmill, built an ox cart for his father, and made numerous mechanical toys. By the age of seventeen he was a master craftsman, and had built many farmhomes in the area, organizing the framing and construction work all himself. He experimented with inventions in other fields and in 1875 patented a new process which he called seamless

▲ La Marcus Adna Thompson, "father" of the gravity roller coaster.

hosiery. Samples were made and sent to the large retail companies in Chicago, the commerce capital of the U.S. at the time. Marshall Field and Company placed an immediate order for $10,000 and that was the beginning of Thompson's famous Eagle Knitting Company which opened in 1877 in Elkhart, Indiana. Six years later turnover was up to $250,000 but Thompson was exhausted and had to take time off.

La Marcus Adna Thompson was one of the tourists who came to ride the Mauch Chunk Switchback in the 1870s when he was supposedly convalescing on doctors' orders after suffering from nervous exhaustion. However, he could never stay idle for long and while on this trip saw the commercial potential of the gravity railway—an amusement park ride that could be built in picnic groves, pleasure gardens, and coastal resorts around the U.S.

Though his idea was not the first to be patented as a roller coaster ride—that title goes to J. G. Taylor and R. Knudson—Thompson's ride was the first to be constructed because neither Taylor's nor Knudson's concepts were built. He was the first to build a roller coaster in a North American amusement park, and justly earned the epithet "Father of the Gravity Ride."

Thompson's Switchback Railway opened in 1884 on Coney Island, Brooklyn, and was an immediate success. It was a crude and simple 5-cent ride, with cars that ran at 6 m.p.h., from a 50-foot high peak on an undulating track by the beach. The track was supported on a wooden structure that was 450 feet long. When the cars reached the bottom of the last dip passengers left the train for attendants to push the cars to the top, where they were switched to the return track for the ride back. It was no scenic

▲ This switchback railway, built at Blackpool, England, in 1904, was designed by Thompson.

▼ A drawing of Thompson's switchback gondola car. Notice the hand grips for the passengers.

▲ A switchback gondola at the Victoria Pleasure Gardens, Burgess Hill, England, in 1909.

26. Looping-The-Loop,
Olentangy Park, Columbus, Ohio

◀ Lina Beecher's Looping The Loop roller coaster ride, built in 1908 at Olentangy Park, California.

Most Wonderful Railway Ever Built for Pleasure Parks

The Centrifugal Cycle Railway
PASSENGERS AND CARS UPSIDEDOWN

IMPOSSIBLE is your first thought. To accomplish the impossible is what is wanted as an attraction. We have accomplished the above feat and at a profit that surpasses the Ferris Wheel, Switchbacks, Roller Coasters, Chutes or Scenic Railways. At Coney Island, N. Y., we are constructing one of these structures for Capt. Paul Boyton. He says "it will be the greatest attraction on the Island and the biggest money-maker."

The first structure of this character was erected in Toledo last year, and after carrying thousands of men, women and children without a single accident, fully demonstrated not only that the law of centrifugal force could

be applied to a railway, but that, with our system regular passenger cars can be run on any grade, around any curve, going to the extreme of throwing a somersault, all without the danger of leaving the track, and this at any attainable rate of speed. The fact is, these cars cannot leave the track. It is a bicycle system and requires but 10 per cent of the usual power.

This road is built upon the Monorail or American Railway system, invented by and bought of Capt. Lina Beecher, Superintendent of this company, who is planning several roads for fast air lines with a speed of two hundred miles an hour.

Contracts filed immediately will insure erection of structures within 30 days. We build and sell outright only.

OSBORN CONGELTON, Pres. and Gen. Mgr.
Capt. LINA BEECHER, Gen. Superintendent. **AMERICAN RAILWAY COMPANY,** 6 WALL STREET, NEW YORK.

◀ An advertisement for an early looping gravity ride, developed by Lina Beecher.

THE L.A.THOMPSON SCENIC RAILWAYS (CONTINENTAL) LTD

NEW YORK,	ST. PETERSBURG,	IN REPLY PLEASE QUOTE
PARIS,	COLOGNE,	
VIENNA,	COPENHAGEN,	
BERLIN,	MOSCOW,	
VENICE,	MALMO.	

TELEPHONE: 1125 REGENT.
TELEGRAMS: "SENICTAL, LONDON."
CODE: WESTERN UNION.

HEAD OFFICES:
26, CHARING CROSS ROAD,
LONDON. w.c.

◀ Letterhead of Thompson's Continental Scenic Railway Company, which was established in 1914 in London.

railway, but it was novel and lots of fun, and people would stand in a line-up for up to three hours to ride it. The 5-cent ride grossed $600 a day.

Thompson's monopoly of the roller coaster ride did not last long. Charles Alcoke of Hamilton, Ohio, designed the first continuous oval ride, without the need for a switchback process, at Coney Island a few months later. This eroded the profits made by Thompson's ride. The Alcoke coaster made a complete circuit in a few minutes with sideways-facing bench seats designed to give passengers better sightseeing views. Other designs soon followed and Thompson knew he had to do something soon to win his market back, but he was not prepared for the impact that Philip Hinckle's new coaster would have on his business. Hinckle's coaster opened in San Francisco in 1885. It was the third coaster to be built in the U.S. It had an elliptical circuit with passengers facing forward in their seats, a hoist to pull the cars to the top of the drop, and it was taller and faster than the other two rides. Hinckle's roller coaster was the first to offer the thrill of the ride, instead of a scenic view of the area. Soon more roller coasters started to appear with faster speeds and greater thrills. In 1887 the Sliding Hill and Toboggan coaster opened in Massachusetts. They were the first to run in a figure-eight loop.

Thompson's response was to establish a roller coaster construction company to sell the rides and ideas that he had patented. Between 1884 and 1887, Thompson was granted over thirty roller coaster patents. With his partner James Griffith he planned, marketed, and built the famous Thompson Scenic Railway. Griffith introduced Thompson to a brilliant young engineer whom they employed as Chief Engineer. His name was John Miller, a man of destiny, who was to dominate roller coaster construction in years to come.

The Scenic Railway was a revolutionary ride combining novelty and new technology. It encapsulated the latest in mechanical devices, it had articulated carriages, a return track, steam powered cables to lift the cars up inclines, but, more importantly, the ride was surrounded by elaborate scenery. There were beautiful grottoes with twinkling colored lights, scenes depicting epic events from history, and tableaux from the Bible which were suddenly flooded by light as the coaster whistled by. It opened on the boardwalk in Atlantic City in 1887 and was soon to become the most popular and famous amusement ride in the world.

Scenic railways spread like wild fire all over the U.S., and were exported to Britain, Europe, and India. Over the years the scenic railway was continually improved on, with more breathtaking scenery and mechanical devices incorporated. In 1909 over eight million people had paid to visit a Thompson ride in the U.S. But the scenic railways' popularity would soon be challenged by a new generation of fast roller coaster rides, like the notorious Drop the Dips, the first of the high-speed coasters, which was built by Christian Feuchts in 1907. Although it burnt down a month later it was rebuilt with a more ferocious drop of 60 feet, and the thrill of the speed circuit proved an immediate success with the public.

Thompson died in 1919 some years after he had completed his masterpiece in Venice,

▲ Entrance to the famous Scenic Railway at Venice Park, California, which opened in 1910.

California, in 1910. It was the first dark ride to be built and was followed many years later by Disneyland's Matterhorn and Magic Kingdom's Space Mountain.

WELCOME TO CONEY ISLAND

The roller coaster and the growth of the amusement park industry are inextricably linked. Without the amusement park, the evolution of the roller coaster would not have occurred, and in Coney Island, at the turn of the century, we see the embodiment of the pleasure park tradition that rings true, even today.

Coney Island was once an idyllic shoreline of sand, of mussel beds, and windblown scrub stretching for five miles along the southern tip of Brooklyn. It was remote and isolated, a place to watch glorious sunsets out at sea. By 1890 it was crowded, noisy, a 24-hour playground of bright lights, brash buildings, carousels, scenic railways, and peep shows—and the amusement mecca of the U.S.

▲ Prescott's Flip Flap Railway, built 1901, was designed with an elliptical curve to reduce the g force at the bottom of the loop.

Horsedrawn streetcars and trolley cars brought people to Coney from Brooklyn. Paddle steamers from Manhattan, on a two-hour journey, ferried people from the city for 50 cents. In 1875 the railway emptied a million passengers into this playland. A year later it had doubled. What was the attraction of the amusement park? Was it the roller coaster, the Ferris wheel, or the lights? Coney Island was an escape for the immigrant worker and the urban working classes, away from the dark and dingy streets, of the squalid living conditions, and overcrowding that prevailed. It was a watering hole for the working classes to come together to enjoy an inexpensive day out. There were silent films, street fairs, and circuses, but Coney Island promises sensory overload, emotional excess, a chance for a boy to meet a girl, a noisy and pulsating arena where you could loose yourself for not much money.

Alongside the pleasure seekers in the early years, came the sleaze, the criminal element, the prostitutes and pimps, the con men and spivs who established themselves down the western end of the beach, which became known as "The Gut." They were tolerated because they paid a fee to the boss of Coney Island, John McKane, a one-man government and self-appointed police chief, who sanctioned land leases, park concessions, and building contracts, rewarding himself and his unsavory friends with the proceeds. His power and influence was so great that it was alleged he rigged the ballots for Presidents Harrison and Cleveland. He was jailed in 1893 for racketeering and this opened up the Island to free enterprise and the building of the first enclosed amusement parks.

How can anyone forget the splendor of Steeplechase Park, Luna Park, and Dreamland on Coney Island? Coney Island was the catalyst for the other great parks such as Cedar Point, historic Kennywood Park, and Blackpool Pleasure Beach in England, where Thompson,

Miller, Baker, Church, and others built their wonder rides. One Coney Island old-timer referred to the coasters that were built on Coney Island during this era as "weeds that popped up as fast as they were torn down."

THE EARLY ENTREPRENEURS

If electricity and the light bulb had not been invented by 1890, Steeplechase Park, Luna Park, and Dreamland could never have existed. They also needed far-sighted, visionary entrepreneurs to make them happen. Coney Island was a fantasy playland, bedazzled with lights that wrapped and draped themselves around every building, artefact, gateway, fence, and amusement ride. It was here that Thompson had installed the first switchback railway and where Captain Paul Boyton opened Sea Lion Park, considered to be the first enclosed amusement park concept with an admission fee. Boyton's Sea Lion Park had forty trained sea lions, water rides including Shoot the Shutes which plunged into the sea lion show pool, and the first commercial looping coaster, named the Flip Flap, designed by Lina Beecher.

The Flip Flap ride at Sea Lion Park seated two passengers and ran by gravity down a hill before wheeling upside-down through a vertical loop at the bottom of the hill. Unfortunately the ride proved quite dangerous and had to be dismantled soon after construction, even though it had been tested with monkeys and sandbags. The tight 25-foot diameter of the loop imparted quite sudden g force on the down section that caused riders to suffer whiplash and other neck injuries. In 1901 Edmund Prescott designed an elliptical curve to a looping coaster to reduce the sudden buildup of g force as the coaster accelerates on the down section. This feature was first introduced on his Loop the Loop coaster on Coney Island.

▲ Welcome to Camelot—the entrance to George Tilyou's Steeplechase Park, Coney Island.

Born near Coney Island, entrepreneur George Tilyou had taken a great interest in the amusement rides like the Thompson Switchback Railway and the carousel as a boy. He had visited the Mauch Chunk Railway and honeymooned at the Great Columbian Exhibition of Chicago in 1894, where he became fascinated by the Ferris wheel. He had bought a large plot of land on Coney Island before he went on honeymoon, to build an amusement park extravaganza he named Steeplechase Park. Every inch of the park was designed to sweep away inhibition and restraint, encouraging extrovert behavior and activity, bringing revelers into innocent but intimate contact with the opposite sex. Tilyou set a one price entrance fee of 25 cents to his fifteen-acre park. Once inside, the patrons could enjoy all the attractions for as long as they wanted. There was the Human Roulette Wheel, the Whirlpool, and the Human Pool Table where whirling carriages whisked and bumped passengers about in all directions.

▲ The eight-lane Steeplechase ride, at Steeplechase Park, was a huge success.

◄ The sensory overload of Luna Park's famous entrance and the exotic eastern influences.

◄ A general view of Luna Park at night, the land of a million light bulbs.

◄ The Dreamland entrance bedecked with replica sculptures, statues, and monumental architecture of classic antiquity.

But the central ride of the park was the Steeplechase from which the park took its name. It was a gravity ride featuring eight wooden horses that raced each other around an undulating eight-lane track. The wooden horses were double saddled to encourage a young lady and young man to ride together. Unlike many of today's fast and furious rides, the steeplechase was a gentle ride that was suitable for all age groups, evoking charm with novelty. By the third year, over a million people had ridden the Steeplechase and its popularity continued for many more years.

Tilyou's brilliance was in designing rides where the patrons were turned into the main attraction. Illusion and fantasy were brought together in a cyclorama show created for Tilyou by Frederick Thompson and Skip Dundy called "Trip to The Moon" in 1901. A year later Thompson and Dundy decided to pull out of Steeplechase Park to set up their own shows and to design a new theme park they named Luna Park, on the site of Boyton's Sea Lion Park which they had acquired for $2 million.

Luna Park opened on the night of May 16, 1903, and was hailed at the time as the greatest concentration of light bulbs and electrical power ever witnessed, with 500,000 light bulbs setting the sky alight that evening. They blazed from monumental towers and twisting minarets, sculptured alabaster animals, fantasy castles, and ornately decorated spires and colonnades. Luna Park's entertainment included the Trip to The Moon, Twenty Thousand Leagues Under the Sea, a boat ride down the Canals of Venice, a Japanese garden, and an Eskimo Village. There were other rides and water features, as well as a daily showing of the Eruption of Vesuvius and the fall of Pompeii. It was a bizarre and fantastic wonderland, giving patrons a flavor of the Orient in a Hollywood setting that could have been used for filming *The Thief of Baghdad*. Thompson and Dundy's Luna Park promised good clean fun in an extravagant setting, plus the added attraction of live entertainment shows.

Luna Park attracted over four million visitors a year in its heyday and it was not until the 1990s that attendance to amusement parks ever matched this statistic. Luna Park closed in 1946 after a devastating fire brought about by a decade of neglect and falling attendance. Steeplechase Park continued to run until the 1960s, but another great park, Dreamland, built shortly after Luna Park, was gutted by a massive fire in 1911—which all of New York came to watch—and never recovered. The Coney Island phenomenon was unique. It was also where the hot dog was invented and, even though nothing remains of the fabulous parks today, it has undoubtedly influenced the design of the modern theme parks—just take a look at Disneyland.

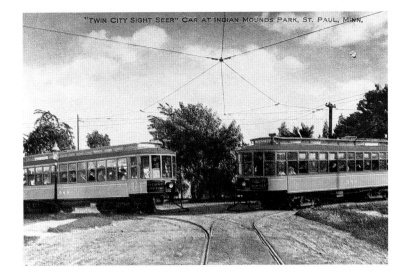

▲ The trolley bus companies and the weekend trolley service were the catalyst for the growth of urban parks and picnic groves.

▶ Street cars transported passengers to trolley parks at the end of the line, like this one at Kennywood Park.

▼ Bathing beauties on the artificial beach of the giant bathing pool at Kennywood Park in the early 1900s.

▲ The Pittsburg Plunge at Lost Kennywood Park today is a replica of the Chute the Shoots ride of the great Luna Park at Cincinnati, in the early 1900s.

▲ Cedar Point, 1890, the Lake Erie shoreline, and the water toboggan ride in the background.

TROLLEY BUS PARKS

The growth of the amusement park, picnic groves, and beach resorts was linked with the trolley bus network and railroad expansion. The companies that built the trolley line and tramways were directly responsible for the establishment of the amusement park as an American institution. As trolley bus companies had to pay for the supply of electricity over the whole week, they found they either had to run a weekend service at a loss or shut down. They built trolley parks and pleasure gardens at the end of the line in an attempt to induce more passengers to ride their trams on the weekend.

Suddenly the weekend service became profitable as more of the public took to the idea of taking a cool tram ride in the summer to get to the park. Trolley bus and tram companies competed with each other for passenger loyalty, building more lavish parks and introducing novel attractions like scenic railways, miniature trains, water shoots, Ferris wheels, and, of course, roller coasters. As business developed, so the bus companies franchised more rides, leased larger sites, acquired more land, and joint ventured with entrepreneurs.

For instance Kennywood Park, considered by many to be the historic roller coaster capital of America, was started by the Monongahela Street Railway Company in 1898. The trolley park they built offered customers band concerts, food, and picnic groves to encourage working people and their families to use the trolley buses for pleasure. Chief Engineer George Davidson, of the Monongahela Railway Company, designed the layout of Kennywood Park. It was such a good design that it has remained largely untouched today, although the park has been greatly extended around it. The original layout featured a large manmade lake dotted with small islands and quaint bridges. The majority of the buildings were well constructed and not cheap mock-ups of plaster and alabaster. There was a dance pavilion, a casino, and carousel building, all interconnected by wide gravel

walkways. The park was planted with hundreds of trees and flowering shrubs which, when they matured, were to grace some of John Miller's great roller coasters—the Pippin, the Racer, and the Jack Rabbit, built in the 1920s. The rides are still operating at Kennywood today, a park where the past is the future, where you can wallow in the nostalgia, and antiquity of many other historic rides like the Tumble Bug, the Denzel Carousel, and the swinging Rocket ride—and enjoy the best French fries and corn dogs in all the U.S.

The amusement park boom was collectively due to Coney Island, the early entrepreneurs, the trolley bus companies, and the new spirit of adventure in the U.S. By the turn of the century, Henry Iles, trading under L. A. Thompson's Scenic Railway Company, was building scenic railways and switchbacks in Great Britain. Rides were also shipped to the Continent and built in Paris, Boulogne, and Barcelona. During this time an Englishman named William Bean, who had spent some years in America in the amusement park industry, was much impressed with what he saw at Coney Island in 1903. He decided to purchase 30 acres of wasteland along the Blackpool shoreline with his partner John Outhwaite. Blackpool Pleasure Beach, as it was to be called, soon became the amusement capital of England and Europe, and one of the great roller coaster parks of the world.

The stage was now set for the roller coaster bonanza of the 1920s. Everything worked together—amusement park owners wanted roller coasters because they were the crowd pullers and king of the rides; roller coaster designers needed lots of permanent sites and orders to build their creations; and park architects wanted a site they could plan for present and future roller coaster rides.

▲ Blackpool Pleasure Beach, England, in 1915 with Thompson's Scenic Railway in the foreground.

▲ The entrance to the Dip the Dips Scenic Railway at Cedar Point in 1908.

▲ Wrecked "Switchback" at Folkestone, Kent,
England, after the storm of October 28, 1906.

THE L. A. THOMPSON SCENIC RAILWAY, VENICE, CALIFORNIA.

▲ Colorful backdrops, mountainous scenery, tunnels, sharp turns, and steep slopes were a feature of the Scenic Railway at Venice Park.

▲ The end of an era, the burning of Ocean Park, California, on September 2, 1912.

LEGENDARY DESIGNERS OF THE ROLLER COASTER

The 1920s was a great time to be living in the U.S. Skyscraper fever was gripping the country, the Gothic splendor of the Woolworth building was standing head and shoulders above every other building on the Manhattan skyline. It was the heyday for the silent film and for stars like Charlie Chaplin and Buster Keaton; it was when Hollywood was created and was soon to become the film capital of the world. It was the machine age where large gas-guzzling limousines pumped toxic fumes into the smog-filled roads, the Wright Brothers had launched the age of flight, and when railroads in the U.S. covered more miles than in all of Europe. It was a time of opportunity and greed; a time when transport magnate J. P. Morgan purchased a big stake in the White Star and Red Star transatlantic liner companies to compete for the lucrative migrant trade, when Al Capone controlled the ganglands of Chicago, and Ku Klux Klan members brutalized the negroes in the south, and sewing machines, vacuum cleaners, and washing machines were being mass produced.

It was an age of discovery and experimentation and the New World was the enterprise capital of the world, where creativity, daring, and entrepreneurial skill were well rewarded. The scenic railway and switchback were just too plodding and pedestrian as rides to match the pace of society. The roller coaster needed to epitomize the speed, adventure,

and recklessness of the times. People wanted excitement and danger, but without doing harm to themselves.

Amusement park owners with their fat check books at the ready, went to market to buy the best rides in the business. Inventors and designers of novelty rides swamped the U.S. patent office with their ideas. A glance at the list of patents for mechanical rides and safety devices from 1900 through 1972 reveals just how many were lodged before 1920. The names of Harry Traver, John Miller, and L. A. Thompson appear frequently; and there was Frederick Church, and James Griffiths. The floodgates were now open, and roller coaster companies were set up to exploit and to supply the rides demanded by the amusement park owners and their public.

Having established itself as an industry in the early 1900s, roller coaster manufacture peaked in the 1920s, with over 2,000 rides, and then collapsed suddenly in the wake of the Wall Street crash, the great depression, and the onset of world war. The boom and bust cycle continued into later decades. There was a revival in roller coaster fortunes in the 50s following the end of the Second World War, then a slow decline into the 70s, followed by another boom into the 80s. The boom continued into the 90s with some 500 roller coasters operating in the world, bucking the trend since the 30s. Moreover

◀ "In the 1920s it seemed everyone owned an automobile"—the parking lot at Kennywood Park, West Mifflin.

forty million visitors today stream into Disney World Resort in Florida every year from all over the world.

Each period of growth in the amusement park industry has set new standards and challenges for the roller coaster. In each boom era there have been the exceptional rides that trail blazed advances in roller coaster engineering, using the materials and technology available in that era.

Who were the greatest roller coaster designers, the legends of their time, and what was so special about the rides they built? There may never be agreement as to who was the greatest, but historians and commentators would have difficulty in disputing the names on the short list that has been drawn up. L. A. Thompson, the "Father of the Gravity Ride," belongs to this elite group, and his story has already been told in the previous chapter. Harry Baker, Andy Vetell, William Cobb, Aurel "Dutch" Vazsin, Joseph Mackee, the brothers Fred and Josiah Pearce, and Charlie Paige have all contributed mightily to roller coaster technology and the amusement park industry in the run up to the 80s, but space has had to limit our choice to the top ten amongst this elite group.

The legends are: John Miller, Frederick Church, Harry Traver, Herbert Schmeck and the PTC, John Allen, Curtis Summers and Charlie Dinn, Karl Bacon and Ron Toomer, and Anton Schwarzkopf. These men were the pioneers of roller coaster engineering and played a significant part in its history from the first 100-foot drop, the invention of the safety ratchet, and underside friction wheel, to the first all-steel, the looping, and the corkscrew coasters. They cover a period from 1920 to the late 70s. In later chapters we take a close look at current trends, the new rides, and the big names that are dominating roller coaster construction today.

JOHN MILLER (1872–1941)

Miller is regarded as the most prolific designer of roller coasters of all time. He started working on amusement rides at the age of nineteen when he secured the position of Chief Engineer for Thompson Scenic Railway Company. He then went on to work for Fred Ingersoll, the Pearce Brothers, Aurel "Dutch" Vazsin, founder of the National Amusement Device Company and the great Philadelphia Toboggan Company, but given the choice he always preferred to work for himself. His inventive mind worked best when he was alone. He set up business partnerships in most cases to help him handle the accounts and finances. His partners were his financial backers and managed his business affairs and the revenues from the rides and inventions that he designed and patented. He held more than fifty patents on roller coaster devices, safety features, and car assemblies. Miller built over a hundred roller coasters in his life time, quite a few of which were hailed as the greatest roller coaster rides ever built. They were all of wooden construction. John Allen, the designer most responsible for the revival of the roller coaster in the 70s, said of Miller's Whirl Wind Coaster built at Olympic Park, New Jersey, in 1924, "For the small

▲ John Miller—pioneer of the wooden roller coaster.

plot of land it occupied, in my opinion, it was the finest roller coaster ever built."

John Miller was born in Homewood, Illinois, a suburb of Chicago, in 1872. His real name was August Meuller, and he appears to be the only child born to his immigrant German parents. Why did he change his name? There is not much written about John Miller's personal life, it remains a mystery, but it is probable it was changed to escape social prejudice at a time when Germany and Britain were at war. He was gifted with an inventive mind and a natural genius to tinker with machinery, to get things to work and function efficiently. He had an innate understanding of the science, of motion, of kinetics, dynamic equilibrium, and centrifugal forces, which he put to use in the development of the roller coaster. Miller pursued his ideas with a single-minded obsession, he was a workaholic who lived and breathed roller coasters every day of his life. Yet, considering the impact his work made, John Miller, the man, remains an enigma. As one of his associates put it: "The rides were the thing, not when or where you were born. We were just too busy putting up rides, and Miller didn't give a damn about [anything else]."

With the safety features that Miller built into his rides, he knew he could design layouts with tighter curves, sharper bends, and steeper drops than any of the competition. And because he had the rights to so many patents which had become design features on all new roller coasters, it was difficult for park owners to avoid having to deal with Miller somewhere along the line. He developed the anti-roll back safety dog, a simple device which prevents cars from rolling backward while being hauled up the slope. It is the cause of the familiar clanking sound as the coaster climbs to the top of the first drop. He also designed the "mega coaster" concept with a long snaking, out and back track, and

▼ Wheels of progress at Euclid Beach Park, Ohio. Miller's Racing Coaster of 1913 is on the left, with steeper drops and higher lift hills than L. A. Thompson's Scenic Railway on the right, built in 1908.

▲ The Racer at Kennywood Park, West Mifflin, 1910.

a first drop of 100 feet which was to emerge in the 70s. Most of the coasters built before 1910 had first drops of not more than 40 to 50 feet and did not travel more than 30 m.p.h., but Miller's was faster, travelling at 55 m.p.h. and started with first drops of between 60 and 100 feet.

His invention of the under friction wheel which he patented in 1910 has been an integral feature of the roller coaster ever since, with hardly any improvements. The under friction wheels stop the car from lifting off the rails as it whips over the top of a curve and from sliding horizontally off the track as the train turns a sharp corner. One set of wheels runs under the rail, and is engaged when the top wheels begin to lift off the track. This will occur only when the upward centrifugal force is greater than the weight

▲ The coaster cars of the Pippin at Kennywood Park in the 1920s.

▶ Miller's patent drawings filed on February 2, 1922, for the wheel arrangement of a coaster car with a dual guide/uplift wheel assembly.

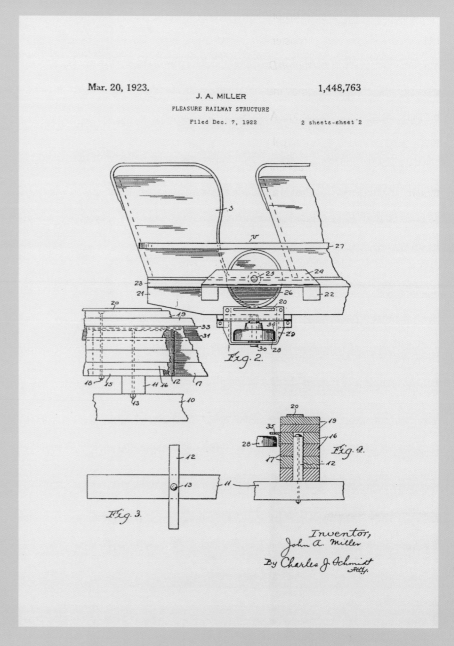

of the car and passengers. Similarly another set of wheels that runs horizontally along the outside of the track becomes engaged when the car beings to slide across the main rail going around a sharp bend. As a result of this and other inventions Miller's roller coaster could be built on smaller sites with reduced land cost—the steep drops and tight bends made it possible. The greater speed, g forces, and thrills that his rides generated made him the most sought after designer in the U.S. at the time.

Where should we begin a short list of John Miller's great coasters? Do we choose one from the Big Dippers, Pippin, Jack Rabbit, Sky Rocket, Deep Dipper, Thriller, Cyclone, and the Racers he designed? Space limitations dictate that the field is narrowed down to a handful of rides. Most enthusiasts would agree that the rides Miller designed through ravines, hugging the undulating landscape of the site, were among his best and Kennywood Park in West Miflin was the setting for three of them.

The Jack Rabbit was built in 1920 for $50,000 when Miller was trading under the partnership of Miller & Baker. Taking advantage of a ravine in which Braddock Spring was located, the scene of an historic battle during the American War of Independence, Miller designed a beautiful coaster layout with an 85-foot double dip, using the barest amount of timber. The *Pittsburgh Despatch* wrote this on the opening day: "Sensational dips, gigantic leaps, dizzy climbs, make the new amusement the most popular attraction between New York and Chicago. A double dip and a long covered passage, in addition to the 85-foot drop, make it a real thriller." It is still operating today.

The Pippin, built in 1924, at Kennywood again, was as successful as his first ride, but this time the coaster was located in a ravine at the opposite end of the park. It was remodeled by Andy Vettel in 1968, retaining the ravine section of Miller's original layout, but adding to the hill section. It has been renamed the Thunderbolt and is now regarded as a classic wooden coaster and one of the great wooden rides of the twentieth century. It is a deceptive ride that catches the rider by surprise as it dips suddenly through the treetops after leaving

◄ "Jack Rabbit Racer," Silver Spray Pier, Long Beach, California. Designed by Ingersoll/Miller, 1915–1929.

▲ The Giant Coaster at Paragon Park, designed in 1910 by Miller for the PTC.

the station. It drops 90 feet rapidly into the ravine before climbing up another slope and plummeting down again. The ride and ravine are cleverly hidden from view by the trees and fence lines that enclose the track.

The Racer was built in 1926 on the site of an old ride which had become dated and obsolete. The Racer was designed with an arched station entrance that was covered in lights and a twin track that delivered a "snappy ride that wasn't too much for mothers and children to ride" declared the park owner Brady McSwigan. It was a beautiful and photogenic ride, but, unlike the Jack Rabbit and Pippin, it did not use the topography of the site. It was built in a hollow with tight banked turns, sweeping curves, and dips.

Other rides that showed the range of Miller's inventive genius include the Dip Lo Do Cus, named after a prehistoric reptile in the Smithsonian, where beautiful shamrock cars produce a whip motion, caused by the deliberately unbalancing load in the car, while traveling over dips and turns along the track. The Flying Turns was strictly a bobsled ride, the invention of Norman Bartlett, who came to Miller to form a partnership to market the ride. The cars ran on rubber wheels along a cylindrical chute made of cyprus wood that spiraled many times on its way down. It was fast and savage, and as lethal a ride as the Cyclone at Palisades Park built by Traver.

Today there are a few Miller coasters still operating. They include the three classic coasters at Kennywood Park, the Geauga Lake Big Dipper, the extended Big Dipper at Blackpool Pleasure Beach, and the Screeching Eagle at Clementon Park, New Jersey. But

▲ The Thunderbolt in the 1970s, the rebuilt Pippin, showing the lift hill halfway round and the ravine drop.

◀ An aerial view of Thunderbolt, with the second half of the ride only visible. The first half drops into a ravine.

Miller's masterpieces were undoubtedly the roller coaster rides through the ravines and none was more exhilarating or more terrifying by first-hand accounts, than the Cyclone he designed at Puritas Springs in Cleveland in 1927. The treetops completely hid this monstrous ride from view. It was only possible to pick out the station and platform as it was approached. The ride is listed in the Smithsonian Institute as one of the Great Lost Roller Coasters.

FREDERICK CHURCH (DIED 1936)

▶ Fred Church.

The Church-Prior partnership and Harry Traver are the names behind the most terrifying and extreme rides ever built—the Cyclones and the Bobs. The jury is still out as to which of their coasters was the most notorious and the most feared because of their "killer" reputation due to the alleged injuries and fatalities that occurred. Society in the roaring 20s was enthused by the speed, power, style, and glamor of the machine age. The amusement park was the arena in which to show off, to be macho, daring, and dangerous; with the high-speed roller coaster providing the ultimate challenge. The arguments still rage on about who built what. Traver was a maverick, an inventive genius, and marketeer, who laid claim to many of the fastest rides ever seen, many of which he did not design. Church designed a lot of the rides that Traver built, although it is a moot point whether it is the designer or the builder who should claim ownership.

▼ Church and Priors Race Thru the Clouds at Venice Lagoon, California, 1911.

There is not a lot in print about Fred Church, the man, and even less has been said about his business partner Thomas Prior. It appears that the archive material on Church was lost with all the Traver documents, when they were destroyed in a fire. Let's then give Church the benefit of any doubt as to ownership, and credit him with the rides that he designed.

When Church and Prior arrived on the scene, roller coaster mania was about to grab the attention of young America. It was the golden era for the amusement park and the roller coaster was the king of the rides, with each park boasting bigger, faster, and more thrilling rides to lure more customers. Besides the magnificent Coney Island Park there was now Euclid Park and the new roller coaster haven of Riverview Park, Olympic Park, the much-loved Crystal Beach, the dramatic seafront setting of Long Beach, the awesome rides at Palisades Park, the fun and froth of Rye Playland, the sensational Revere Beach, and many others. These parks had to be experienced to be believed. The old photographs can only give a hint of the dangerous turns and twists of the coaster soaring high on the skyline.

Like Miller before him, Fred church was a quiet man, gifted with practical good sense and an analytical mind, who also patented and improved the design of the coaster car for many years to come. He developed the two-wheel trailer cars, coupled by a ball and socket joint to give each car individual articulation. The design was necessary so that the cars could negotiate the severe turns and banked curves in his rides.

▲ The awesome and thrilling Cyclone at Revere Beach, Massachusetts, built 1925.

Church had the gift and vision to know what was wanted by his patrons. He designed probably some of the greatest wooden coasters of all time, and was the designer and inspirational guru of the Church-Prior partnership. Prior was the business man, the accountant, and financial wizard. The partnership worked very well, with Church developing over a hundred roller coaster rides in his time. They also patented the Derby Racer carousel, the first of which opened in Steeplechase Park. Only three remain in operation today: at Cedar Point, Blackpool Pleasure Beach, and Rye Playland.

Church worked for many years in Venice, California, from an office set up very close to the entrance to one of his rides, Race Thru The Clouds, at Venice Amusement Park. It was from this office that he doodled and sketched the phenomenally successful and thrilling layout of the Airplane Coasters and the Bobs, with their steep drops, writhing turns, and acutely angled curves. Later luminaries, like John Allen and Andrew Vettel—both successful designers in the 60s—can remember getting nose bleeds riding the Airplane Coaster as young lads. How severe or bruising was it? Here is an extract of what Louis Bottle wrote in the *Sunday News Magazine* in 1937.

"The Airplane Coaster was 92 feet high and was constructed in a series of curves. When the car reached the top of the first hill and started its descent, it took a sharp curve then plunged straight down into a tunnel ten feet below ground. That was nothing. The second hill was built like a whirlpool. At the top, the car made an immediate curve, then reached down a spiral track banked so steeply that you were thrown to one side, rattled and knocked almost senseless as it shook the breath out of you. The rest of the ride consisted of shattering drops and twists. We were never able to ride the coaster twice in succession. It jangled your nerves so that you had to recuperate on the carousel."

The Airplane was situated in the center of the beautifully landscaped gardens and Art Deco architecture of Rye Playland, New York. Church had been hired to build a series of coasters at Playland for $200,000 and that was no small sum considering that in 1928 the 273-acre park had cost $5 million to develop. One coaster was a junior ride for children. Another was a smooth scenic coaster, with gentle dips and smooth turns,

▲ Ride ticket for the Cyclone, Revere Beach.

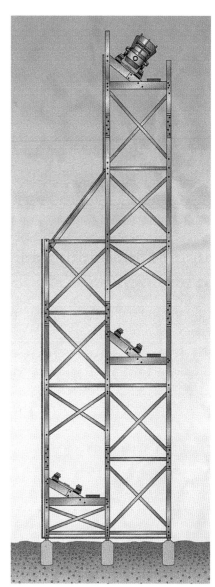

▲ The support structure of the Airplane Coaster, with the track weaving in and out of the towering wooden framework.

◀ The spectacular and towering Airplane Coaster at Rye Playland, New York, 1933.

"If you can ride the 'BOBS' you're good for a 100."

▲ An advertisement for Church's much-loved Belle Vue Bobs, Manchester, England, in the 1930s.

for the family to ride. This was probably the famous Dragon Coaster. And the third was the high-speed Airplane Coaster.

The track of the Airplane was about 3,500 feet long, and it generated a top speed of 40 m.p.h., which is not terrifying by todays standards, but as it was built on a compact site, the compressed layout of the track brought the massive walls of the timber superstructure much closer together, giving the illusion of traveling through avenues of trees at great speed and with viscous acceleration. After the initial plunge, the cars banked through a series of tight spirals, then catapulted out along a low section enclosed in a tunnel before speeding along a series of unexpected dips and turns. It was the overpowering presence of the timber structure so close to the track that created the unrelenting sensation of speed all through the ride. This could explain why there were so few repeat rides. The wide base and tapering top of the timber trusses framing the 180 degree turns at either end of the track, gave the structure an esthetic symmetry and "bottleneck" look that was so unique to the Airplane Coaster.

The ride was sensational by night, with the silhouette of the track picked out by illuminations dotted along the dips and turns. The coaster overlooked Long Island Sound, its bottleneck structure standing high on the skyline acting as a beacon for yachts and boats out at sea.

The Bobs, Riverview Park, Illinois

Somewhere between the DeVry Institute of Technology's parking lot, the Riverview Plaza shops, and the River North lies the former site of the Bobs—a piece of American history

▶ The beautifully maintained "Giant Dipper" at Santa Cruz Boardwalk was copied from a Church design, and built by Arthur Looff in 1924.

that will remain in the hearts and minds of Chicagoans and coaster fans the world over. Riverview Park is gone, the site demolished, and nothing remains of the rides that made this one of the great parks of the Mid West, with two million visitors a year in the 60s. It is now covered by a shopping mall, a police precinct, an industrial park, and an education establishment. But once it was the site of the ultimate roller coaster.

▼ The giant Dipper Bobs, situated at Venice Pier, California, 1924.

Carl Beske was operations manager of the Bobs for twenty-two glorious years. His office was near the back of the station, and in one of the cupboards was an amazing collection of false teeth, spectacles, wallets, and a satin-lined jewel box. The jewel box contained seven thousand earrings, worth a small fortune in gold and silver plate. These, along with the false teeth, spectacles, and wallets, had fallen out of the Bobs during the ride and were found beneath the superstructure. This collection gave the ride an extra dimension in fear and terror.

It was alleged that those who rode the Bobs seldom rode any other ride at Riverview Park. It had all the drama, speed, and thrill of all the other rides rolled into one. The 3,300-foot track layout was not smooth, nor esthetic in construction; it was ragged and twisting with not a hint of straight or level track to give the rider any respite. The train hurtled left and right through twelve curves, dipped and climbed sixteen hills, turned several horseshoe curves, snaked along two crossovers, shaking and rattling the rider from side to side all the way round. It had a top speed of 60 m.p.h., a first drop height of 87 feet, which was inclined at 55 degrees and a ride duration of 2 minutes and 10 seconds. It was a safe ride, although there was one fatality when a man was flung onto the track below and run over by another train. He stood up at the top of the slope to wave at his family and was knocked out of the coaster by the sign that warned him not to stand up.

▲ Twenty-year-old student Vance Tutton sets a world record of 325 nonstop circuits on the Belle Vue Bobs, Manchester, England, August 1967.

Every brake and control of the entire track was operated electrically from a central control tower which had a clear view over the whole track. Should a train fail to clear a section of track in a given time, the next train entering the section would have all its brakes set off automatically. There were three trains operating on the track at any time, and each train consisted of eleven cars carrying twenty-two passengers. In its lifetime the Bobs thrilled over thirty million people.

Today only the graceful lines of the Giant Dipper at Belmont Park, San Diego, and the Coaster at Western Washington Fair are left to remind us of the legendary Fred Church.

► Ride ticket for the famous Bobs at Riverview Park, Chicago.

▶ Harry Guy Traver—a legend in terror.

▼ Traver's Circle Swing ride that brought him and his company many years of financial success.

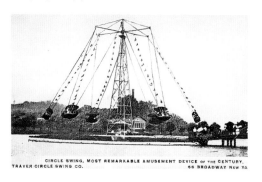

CIRCLE SWING, MOST REMARKABLE AMUSEMENT DEVICE OF THE CENTURY.
TRAVER-CIRCLE SWING CO.   66 BROADWAY NEW YO

▲ The Tumble Bug at Euclid Beach. A few still survive to this day.

HARRY G. TRAVER (1877–1961)

Magician or maverick, a man of destiny and vision, or a con man with an inventive mind and persuasive personality, or a naïve idealist with no head for business. This is what has been said about Harry G. Traver, legendary builder of the most terrifying roller coaster rides of the 20s and 30s. Traver was one of seven children and was born in Gardner, Illinois, on November 25, 1877, on the farm of his father Egbert William and mother Marion (Easton) Traver. His paternal ancestors were German, and emigrated in 1710 to settle in Rhinebeck, New York.

It is difficult to imagine what inspired Traver to design, on the one hand, the intricate and novel mechanical rides for children and the family, and, in complete contrast, the menacing speed machines that terrified people. His passion for machines and mechanical devices and the Jekyll and Hyde character of his creations did not emerge till later in his formative life. He was twenty-one, earning a pittance, and bored with teaching social history at the local high school in Nebraska when he decided to join the General Electric Company as a trainee mechanical engineer. He worked his apprenticeship with GEC on the 1898 Omaha Exposition. The inspiration for his future obsession was undoubtedly fostered by his involvement with electrical machinery, tramways, and the first mechanical fire engine which he later worked on with the Harris Safety Company in 1901.

But the turning point in his life came quite by chance as he lounged lazily on board a cattle boat heading for Europe, convalescing from an illness. As he sat in the deck chair, looking up at the sky watching seagulls effortlessly circling the ship's mast, he struck on an idea for an amusement ride. On his return to New York in 1901, he set about designing and building his first amusement park ride, the Circle Swing.

It was the forerunner of the many rides that he invented over the years, such as the Tumble Bug, the Butterfly, and the Merry Mix—all novelty rides for the family. And it preceded the bruising roller coaster rides of terror that became the Traver hallmark. Those awesome, twisting, curving walls of steel and wood that attracted huge crowds—more to watch than ride—are revered today by both connoisseurs of the roller coaster and roller coaster enthusiasts, and acclaimed as the ultimate scream machine.

The Traver Circle Swing Co in New York designed and built his first ride, the Circle Swing, and lived off the earnings from the ride for several years. Traver earned a good living selling rides to parks. He soon designed other novelty rides and worked on the repair and redesign of other manufacturer's rides. It is likely this is how he came in contact with the prolific roller coaster designer Fred Church and his partner Prior, and this sparked off a deep interest in roller coaster engineering.

He concentrated on building up his company, increasing turnover, selling lots of novelty rides, and looking out for land and bigger premises to expand the business. He met the most important person in his life, the diminutive Ruth Correll, in 1917 at Luna Park, Coney Island, where he was assembling a new ride. She was at the park with her aunt and noticed the energetic Traver supervising the construction of the Butterfly. Their eyes met and the chemistry started. It did not take Traver long to propose to her, to establish his second family with Ruth, and build a brand new home in Beaver Falls.

Although the Butterfly was a failure and dismantled within two years, Traver had by now acquired a permanent factory in Beaver Falls, and renamed his company the Traver Engineering Company. The new site was bought in 1919 in partnership with his close friend Hilary Ackley, with a cash capital of $8,200. Turnover had risen from $300,000 to $400,000 per year, and, despite the $13\frac{1}{2}$-acre site Traver had obtained, there was only sufficient spare capacity to turn out just two roller coasters a year. Numerous novelty rides were also being supplied to amusement parks around the world.

By 1920 the Traver Engineering Company was regarded by everyone in the business as the world's largest amusement ride manufacturer, turning out around 2,000 different rides every year. Without exception if there was a major fair or exhibition held somewhere in the world at least one of Traver's rides would be on display.

But it was the roller coaster that gained Traver his legendary status. In order to diversify and expand the business, he negotiated a contract with the famous roller coaster company of Church and Prior, to construct their roller coasters—all of which were of timber construction. The Traver Engineering Company built the fabulous Belle Vue Bobs, the Cyclone at Revere Beach, and the Thunderbolt at Saven Rock, Connecticut, for Fred Church, which was arguably among the greatest wooden rides ever built.

His interest in the roller coaster turned into a personal crusade as the public and amusement park owners found the roller coaster to be the most exciting and profitable ride in the parks. A number of engineering companies climbed on the bandwagon to exploit this lucrative market, offering better and faster roller coaster rides. Traver realized he had to design something a little more daring, and a little different if his designs were going to be the best in the field. He set about redesigning the Church and Prior toboggan, and reducing friction by making them heavier and longer so that they would travel continuously at speeds of 60 m.p.h. As a result he was able to incorporate sheer drops, high banked curves, and tight turns and twists on his track layout, that generated forces approaching 3 g at high speed. His design could withstand the buffeting and pounding

▲ The structure of the viscous Cyclone coaster at Crystal Beach, Ontario, Canada, built 1927.

▼ The intense turns of the track of Cyclone generated large horizontal g forces.

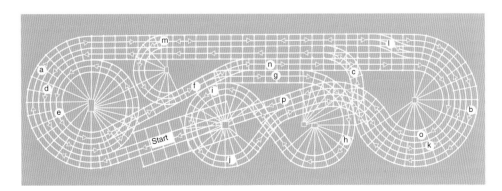

◀ Plan of the track layout of Cyclone at Crystal Beach: (a) station (b) lift approach (c) chain incline (d) highest point (e) initial descent into spiral dip (f) second hill and sharp left turn (g) drop (h) spiral approach (i) tight spiral (j) trim/emergency brake (k) drop (l) high-speed figure-eight (m) drop (n) return under lift hill (o) camel humps (p) final high-speed turn (q) zigzag section.

▲ The frighteningly twisted track of the Lightning coaster at Revere Beach, built 1927.

▲ Probably the most terrifying roller coaster ride ever built. Lightning closed after only a few years because of its killer reputation.

of the 5-ton dynamic force that was torpedoed down the track because he built his support structure in steel. He believed that a steel structure was far stronger and safer than a wooden structure, and he was right.

He pioneered and built the first all-steel roller coaster structure in the world, and he was also the first man to use aluminum to build lighter and longer toboggans to increase the pay load and reduce the long-term maintenance. Although the Cyclone Coaster was the name first used by Church on his designs, the name Cyclone became synonymous with Traver coasters over the years.

Traver built one of the most terrifying and majestic roller coasters of the day, the Cyclone at Crystal Beach, Ontario. It was 96 feet high with a track length of just under 3,000 feet and at night it was illuminated by 1,000 incandescent light bulbs. The ride duration was short, at 40 seconds, but the layout on the confined site was packed with steep gradients and knife-edge turns. It started off with a frightening first plunge designed as a spiral dip, followed by an extremely tight and twisting second spiral dip. It was the only coaster ever built to have a nurse on duty at the unloading platform! His other illustrious coaster design was the Lightning at Revere Beach, Massachusetts, which had a fatality on its debut in 1926 when a girl fell to her death and the ride had to be stopped for 20 minutes so that her body could be removed. The Cyclone Racer at Long Beach, California, is the other Traver special with two tracks laid side by side so that the toboggans could race each other all the way to the finish. It had a dramatic setting built on a pier over the sea and was a landmark for miles around. It was built in 1930 and demolished in 1968, and was hailed as the greatest ride on earth at the time.

As suddenly as Traver had shot to success his company was made bankrupt by the recession that hit America. In 1933, without a penny left, he took his family to England to build amusement park rides in partnership with Leonard Thompson for the Blackpool Pleasure Beach and other pleasure parks in Europe. He was never to return to his glory days, nor to build any more terrifying coaster rides with the exception of one last attempt at Blackpool. The Grand National roller coaster, considered by many to be the finest and most thrilling roller coaster ride in Europe for many decades and still operating today, was built in 1935 as a copy of the Cyclone Racer at Long Beach. Charlie Paige, another legend of the roller coaster, is credited with its construction but there is no doubt that he was given considerable advice from Traver while they were both under contract to Leonard Thompson at Blackpool.

Traver returned to America just before the start of the Second World War and made a modest living working in the amusement park industry and designing novelty rides. He died in 1961 aged 84 at New Rochelle, New York.

▲ The evocative silhouette of the Cyclone Racer, considered one of the finest wooden roller coaster rides of its day.

◄ Constructing the Grand National at Blackpool Pleasure Beach, 1935. Its layout and design was based on the Cyclone Racer.

The Traver Hall Of Fame

Cyclone, Crystal Beach, Ontario (built 1926, demolished 1948) The 36-inch gauge track was constructed of laminated wood with 3 x $^1/_2$-inch flat steel rails screwed into the wood to carry the cars. The support structure was built of 250 tons of prefabricated steel and 20,000 feet of Colombian fir, held together by several tons of spikes, bolts, screws, and nails. The ride was advertized as "the world's largest, fastest, safest, and most thrilling ride." Nothing could be closer to the truth.

Depending on the daily attendance, three to five cars were used for each ride, with twelve to twenty passengers per train. The track started with an 80-degree incline to the first drop—the drop that made women faint and men scream in terror. After the first drop, the coaster turned a spiral that was extremely tight and finished in a figure eight, turning over and under itself to disorient its passengers.

Cyclone Racer, Pike, Long Beach, California (built 1930, demolished 1968) It was a beautiful esthetic structure, with a dramatic setting built out over the sea, supported on a long pier. It opened on Memorial Day on May 30, 1930, and was built at a cost of $140,000. Public reaction to the fearful looking attraction was immediate—it was love at first sight, with attendances soaring to new heights.

The Cyclone Racer was 96 feet high and over 110 feet above the beach. The first drop measured 90 feet at a 50-degree angle and gave the five toboggan trains a top speed of 60 m.p.h. The double track had an elaborate figure eight that cascaded at three different levels, allowing alternate trains to take the lead on the inside of the turns, making a very sporting and exciting ride. The Cyclone Racer was run on two separate tracks without any crossovers, with a ride duration of 105 seconds, and track length measuring 3,400 feet. It was not as terrifying as other Traver designs, but its unique location made it a popular backdrop for many Hollywood movies, and its character made it the most visited roller coaster in the world. It held the record for the most passengers riding a roller coaster in a year at 1,400,000, a record which stood until the 1970s.

HERBERT P. SCHMECK (1890–1956)

The Philadelphia Toboggan Company, PTC for short, founded in 1904 by Chester Albright and Henry Auchy, is the longest running roller coaster company in the world and the name most associated with the roller coasters in the first golden era. The PTC dominated the roller coaster market in the 20s and 30s. Many great designers worked for PTC, including Joe McKee, John Miller, John Allen, and builders like William Strickler, but it was Herb Schmeck who must be given credit for bringing the company success in the highly competitive years of the 20s and 30s—the years that John Miller, Church and Prior, Harry C. Baker, and Harry Traver were trail blazing.

▲ Herb Schmeck.

Schmeck joined PTC as a construction engineer straight from college. He was promoted to construction supervisor and worked under John Miller and William Strickler, building the Giant Coaster at Paragon Park, which he went on to manage. In the early 1920s he supervised the construction of numerous PTC coasters designed by Miller. He had to travel the length and breadth of the U.S., staying in boarding houses and living out of a suitcase. He was an able administrator, an excellent man manager, and good at handling money and contracts.

In three years he had supervised the construction of ten major riders and knew every phase of the work, from the design layout, the foundation and structure, through test runs. But while Miller was still available, Auchy, the president of PTC would not trust young Schmeck with the design so he had to wait till Auchy died to get his chance. His first coaster was for Hershey Park and was built in 1923. It was one of the most profitable rides PTC had

▲ The toboggan car designed by Schmeck for the PTC.

ever built, so that even during the Depression of 1929 through 1938 the ride made money for the company. He designed several coasters between 1924 and 1925 but none as exciting as the Wildcat and Twister at Coney Island, Cincinnati.

He used fancy curves and airplane dips in its figure-eight layout. The track did not have a straight section except at the loading platform. The smaller of the two coasters, the Twister, had a completely covered track from beginning to end. The cars were beautifully fabricated with oak and white pine. The cars had drop forge steel tractor wheels and frames, with deep springs to give a comfortable ride.

The following year PTC received a contract to design two coasters for Woodside Park in Philadelphia. Again one was a large design by Schmeck—the Wildcat—with an 80-foot first drop, and the other was the Tornado, a smaller covered ride with a 52-foot drop. These two rides created the stock design for the PTC stable and sold year after year because of their proven drawing power. This helped to establish PTC as one of the top suppliers of roller coasters in the U.S.

Schmeck was never named as the designer of PTC coasters. The corporate philosophy of the company was to suppress the name of the individual for the good of the company. Yet he was responsible for the design and construction of 210 roller coasters, as well as numerous Funhouses, Tunnels of Love, Water Chutes, and Cuddle-Up rides. He was made president of the company in the 40s and guided PTC profitably through into the 50s when he handed over to his understudy, John Allen. Of the Schmeck designs still operating today there is the Comet at Hershey Park (1946), Joyland's Roller Coaster (1949), the rebuilt 1948 Comet at Great Escape, Lake George, and the classic and much loved Phoenix at Nobles Amusement Resort formerly the Rocket (1947) at San Antonio Playland.

▲ The Comet at Crystal Beach, Ontario, was built over the footprint of Traver's Cyclone after it was dismantled.

◄ The Phoenix at Knoebels Park, Pennsylvania, was formerly the Skyrocket designed by Schmeck. It was moved from Joyland Park, Texas, and rebuilt by Charlie Dinn.

The Second Golden Age of the Roller Coaster

By the 60s the great coasters of the 20s and 30s were all but demolished, the empty tills had closed many of the rides. The affluent middle classes, the major patrons of the city-based amusement parks, had moved out of the city to live in the leafy suburbs and had turned to television for their entertainment in the comfort and safety of their homes. The blacks and poor migrant population of Hispanic and other nationalities replaced them in the city.

These were the new customers of city center amusement parks, who vandalized and indirectly bankrupted many of the amusement parks that burgeoned near the towns and city centers. Olympic Park, for example, was ransacked, smashed, and looted by five hundred rampaging youths in May 1965. The area had become a hang-out for gangs who regularly targeted the rusting rides for their own sadistic fun. The owners closed the park and sold the site to developers shortly afterward. The out-of-town parks, no longer served by trams or trolley buses, and only accessed by the car, like Cedar Point, Kennywood Park, Hershey Park, and Knotts Berry Farm, managed to survive largely because they had the space for large parking lots.

It was at this low point that the phenomenon that was to change the fortunes of the amusement park industry opened in the groves of Anaheim, California. Disneyland, the creation of Walt Disney, captured the imagination of all America and the world almost overnight. The theme park concept had arrived, people were lining up at the turnstiles again, and heralding the dawn of a second golden era of the roller coaster. Disney was the savior of the amusement park industry which has continued to flourish from that opening day on July 17, 1955.

Lowell Thomas and Merian Cooper's Cinerama film, introduced in 1952, with three cameras projecting images simultaneously onto a big screen, was the movie sensation of the year. It featured the Atom Smasher designed by Vernon Keenan at Rockaway Beach in the opening sequences. So vivid and exciting was the virtual reality of the ride, that it revived interest in the roller coaster almost immediately.

In this era of great design, two distinct schools of ideas emerged whose rivalry was to create a coaster war. There was the Wood Revivalists School, followed by those who wanted to reincarnate the fabulous wooden coasters of Miller, Church, and Traver. Included in their number were John Allen, and Curtis Summers and Charlie Dinn. Then there was the Steel Innovators Club, who rejected the old ideas and designed exclusively in steel to set new trends in coaster design, delivering sensational high-speed rides. They included Ron Toomer and Karl Bacon, and Anton Schwarzkopf.

◄ Looking down the first drop of the Phoenix.

The 1952 Cinerama presentation *This is Cinerama* features a ride on the Atom Smasher, a wooden coaster built in 1939.

John Allen standing in front of Screamin' Eagle at Six Flags Over Mid-America.

JOHN ALLEN (1907–1979)

Allen became president of the Philadelphia Toboggan Company in 1954, and the future head for the company until he died, serving his apprenticeship with the company in his youth under Herb Schmeck. The PTC and, to a lesser extent, the National Amusement Devices Company were the two companies responsible for keeping the industry from total extinction during the years of depression. The PTC was without question the most celebrated coaster company from the 30s through the 70s, and attracted the best and most gifted engineers. That's why Allen joined.

Allen is the man credited with starting the coaster boom of the 70s, a boom that began with the opening of his Kings Island Racer in Cincinnati on April 29, 1972. This ride is considered by many coaster buffs to be one of the most esthetic and graceful wooden coasters ever built. It was the first major ride of its time to be televized, and made the six o'clock news on its opening day. Word spread so fast that the roller coaster became part of many TV commercials and starred in the film *Roller Coaster* with Richard Widmark and George Segal.

John Allen was born in Philadelphia on May 21, 1907 and died there in 1976. He went to Drexel University to study engineering but was told that he would not make it

▲ The illustrious Racer at Paramount's Kings Island, Ohio.

▼ First drop of Screamin' Eagle at Six Flags Over Mid-America.

▲ Mr Twister at Elitch Gardens before it was moved. It was the most celebrated of John Allen's Wooden coasters.

as an engineer. He started with the PTC as a junior at the bottom of the ladder operating PTC coasters at Holyoke, Massachusetts, where he studied their workings and learnt intuitively about their engineering. He soon became the company's main troubleshooter, sorting out problems with PTC rides all over the U.S. One of his more interesting troubleshooting jobs was to assist Herb Schmeck in dismantling Traver's legendary Crystal Beach Cyclone in 1947, using much of its timber and steel bracing in order to build the illustrious Comet.

Over the next twenty-five years, this elegant, quietly spoken man designed a dozen more coasters. He was of the Wood Revivalist School and it was his ideas that led to the "mega" coaster concept. Among his celebrated designs are the Great American Scream Machine at Six Flags Over Georgia, The Screamin' Eagle at Six Flags Over Mid America, Twister at Elitch Gardens, Blue Streak at Cedar Point, and, of course, the glorious Kings Island Racer. His designs worked on the symmetry and flow of the track, on the harmony and equilibrium of the ride, not the delivery of terrorizing speed and savage drops. The geometrical proportion, alignment, and esthetic of the superstructures he designed were modeled so exquisitely that they were turned into an art form, a sumptuous piece of working sculpture on a grand scale. His rides were smooth and effortless, lacking the

▲ Summers and Dinn's Predator at dusk, with the distinctive humps of the coaster clearly visible in the reflections in the lake.

▲ Curtis Summers standing on the right, with Charlie Dinn at an I.A.A.P.A. convention in 1989.

punch and brutalism perhaps of the 20s rides, but providing fun for all the family.

His favorite coaster was the Screamin' Eagle, built in 1976, and at the time it was the longest and tallest roller coaster in the world with a track length of 3,872 feet, maximum height of 110 feet, and a top speed of 62 m.p.h. It was a tame ride according to coaster buffs, but John Allen was not designing coasters just for a handful of macho enthusiasts to enjoy, he was building them for the masses of ordinary folk who came to the park. His one extreme ride was Twister built at Elitch Gardens in 1964 and revamped by him in 1965 because it was deemed to run too slow. It was turned into one of the great wooden rides of the day, with a continuous twisting layout that spiraled its way dizzily to the bottom, at great speed. It was, sadly, demolished in 1995 when the whole of Elitch Gardens was moved to a new location. Twister II, built by the Pierce Corporation in the new Elitch Gardens, is a copy of Allen's Twister but it's just not as good as the original.

Curtis Summers (1929–1992) and Charlie Dinn (1933–)

The Summers-Dinn dynasty did not emerge until the late 80s. Until then Curtis Summers, a brilliant Ohio structural engineer, had set up in practice designing the support structures for coaster manufacturers like PTC. He was engaged by the Taft Corporation to design many of the buildings, including the 330-foot replica of the Eiffel Tower, that can be seen at Kings Island today. He worked with John Allen on the Kings Island Racer, and designed the support structures of many of the best wooden rides like Grizzly at Kings

Dominion, Wilde Beast and Minebuster at Canada's Wonderland, and one of the all-time greats, and a favorite of coaster buffs, the Texas Giant for Six Flags Over Texas, Arlington.

Summers developed a computer program for monitoring the changes in the g force, the speed of travel, and centrifugal forces acting on the coaster, the track, and the support framework. The structures he designed were framed in steel or timber, always elegant in construction, slender in mass, and cost effective to build.

Charlie Dinn was working as construction manager for Kings Island Corporation, building the Beast, when he was invited to supervise the relocation and rebuilding of the San Antonio Rocket designed by Schmeck in 1946 for the PTC. The new site was Knoebels Amusement Park and the ride was going to be renamed the Phoenix. The Rocket relocation sparked off a tremendous enthusiasm amongst park owners for restoring and rebuilding old wooden coasters. Dinn's success at this work eventually allowed him to set up his own company to do just that. He rebuilt and restored fourteen wooden rides, and relocated the Giant Coaster from Paragon Park to Wild World and the Skyliner from Roseland to Lakemont Park.

Dinn approached Summers to redesign the superstructure of the relocated Rocket and this forged the beginnings of a collaboration that lasted for many years. The restoration business soon developed into ideas for new rides, featuring muscular coaster rides that stretched for almost a mile, that sped over lakes, dipped through trees, hurtled down gorges, and overpowered every other park structure as far as the eye could see. These were the reincarnations of the awesome, white knuckle rides of Traver, and Church and Miller, only they were faster and bigger. The trains were light and fast, the aluminum track was smooth yet twisting, and the huge timber framework that supported the writhing layouts was a monumental forest of raking pikes in a fortress of timber defences. They were not the refined, esthetic designs of John Allen, but brutal, uncompromising configurations that were not intent on trying to look pretty. Park owners bathed in the profits and public interest that followed the Summers-Dinn coaster output.

They were the coaster gurus of the 80s, each design a "call bird" for the park, an advertisement beckoning customers to ride. Summers and Dinn built thirty-two coasters during their collaboration; many of them are the top wooden rides in the U.S. today. For example, there are rides like Hercules at Dorney Park, built out over a lake with a first drop of 157 feet heading straight down toward the water; or Predator at Darien Lake, New York, a visually dramatic out and back coaster layout that coils its way along the edge of the lake; or the terrifying timber configuration of Mean Streak at Cedar Point located in a flat bowl of land to heighten the drama of the ride to come; or the seven-acre footprint of Timber Wolf at World of Fun delivering nearly 3 g, as it plummets the dips and screams round hairpin turns.

▲ The long snaking outward run of Predator at Darien Lake.

▼ The all-wooden structure of Raging Wolf Bobs built by Summers and Dinn in 1988, at Geauga Lake, Ohio.

◀ Charlie Dinn (left) standing next to his daughter Denise Dinn-Larick, her husband, and brother.

▶ The massive structure of Mean Streak at Cedar Point.

▲ The Corkscrew at Cedar Point, another Arrow invention for a steel coaster ride, designed by Ron Toomer, 1975.

▲ Ron Toomer (left) with a colleague at Blackpool Pleasure Beach at the opening of The Pepsi Max Big One, 1994.

The Dinn-Summers collaboration dominated the coaster market in the 80s. Summers parted company with Dinn in 1991, and died a year later but not before he had worked with Intamin AG to design the Pegasus at Efteling Park in Holland and Japan's first wooden coaster, the Jupiter. Dinn retired from active roller coaster construction in 1991, the year that his collaboration with Summers broke up and his company was dissolved. He now works as a consultant for Custom Coaster International (CCI), the most successful wooden coaster manufacturers in the world today. The company is run by his daughter Denise Dinn-Larrick, her husband Richard, and his son Jeff Dinn.

RON TOOMER (1930–) AND KARL BACON (1910–)

Karl Bacon, along with Edgar Morgan and Walter Schulze, founded the Arrow Dynamics Company in 1946, but he alone invented the tubular steel track coaster which is the basis for all modern steel coasters. He designed the first tubular steel track ride for the Matterhorn Bobsleds at Disneyland in 1959. He developed the log flume ride and came up with the idea of a corkscrew steel roller coaster in 1968.

Karl Bacon established Arrow Dynamics as the foremost and longest-running steel coaster manufacturer in the world. Working closely with Walt Disney's imagineers—who had approached Arrow to design and build a series of new and innovative rides—Arrow helped Disneyland become a reality and a success to both organisations. The name Arrow Dynamics today is to steel coasters what the PTC was to the wooden coasters in the 20s and 30s. The company introduced a new language to the roller coaster world through the many outstanding rides it pioneered in steel—the corkscrew, reverse point shuttle loops, mine trains, suspended, multi-inversion, and the steel hyper coasters of the 90's.

The Arrow hallmark has always been design innovation. The company wants to be first, to be ahead of the competition; its "can do" philosophy concentrates on smoothness of ride, a fast and safe track, low maintenance, and long service record. Karl Bacon needed a brilliant engineer to put together the concepts and ideas that he had, and also someone who could dream up some good ideas in addition to keeping the Arrow flag flying in the future.

Ron Toomer, the former chairman and now consultant director of Arrow Dynamics, joined Arrow in 1965 after being displaced from the aerospace industry. Bacon wanted a mechanical engineer to help design the first Runaway Mine Train, which was to be built at Six Flags Over Texas the next year.

In a letter to me written on November 6, 1997, Toomer recalls the early years of growing up and working with Karl Bacon.

"Karl Bacon was born somewhere in the eastern U.S., as I recall him telling me about his trip to California as a small boy with his family and the many problems with cross-country travel by automobile. Karl always talked about his interest in machinery at a young age and in growing up on the farm. During the Second World War he worked as a tool and die maker in a factory in Sunnyvale, California, where he met Ed Morgan who was an industrial engineer. When the war ended they found themselves out of work and decided to open a job shop to make whatever anyone needed at the time. All of this led into manufacturing some very basic kiddie rides, carousels, and a collaboration with Walt Disney which established Arrow Dynamics. Karl was a self-made engineer, with no formal engineering education, and was one of the best engineers I have ever known."

After the mine train, Toomer went on to design the first corkscrew coaster at Knott's Berry Farm in 1975. He and his team of engineers then developed the idea of a suspended coaster, where the rider is strapped into a car that is suspended from tubular rails, to give the ride the feeling of being airborne as it swings through banked turns. The prototype for the ride was the Bat at Kings Island. It was a disaster and was dismantled after two years amid numerous mechanical problems. But the lessons were learnt the hard way, and the initial financial losses were slowly recovered. The multi-inversion Vortex designed by Arrow immediately replaced the Bat at Kings Island and was a great success.

▼ The multi-inversion Vortex designed by Arrow immediately replaced the Bat at Kings Island and was a great success.

▲ Viper at Darien Lake, with its boomerang section and helix turns, was Arrow's extension of the looping coaster pioneered by Schwarzkopf.

▲ Big Thunder Mountain, a copy of the Matterhorn Bobsled, the first steel track roller coaster in the world. Designed for Disney by Karl Bacon, 1959.

▶ The sinuous structure of Orient Express expresses the dramatic sculptural and esthetic qualities of a steel coaster.

▲ The hyper coaster concept was a world beater for Arrow. The Pepsi Max Big One, seen here, was cloned from Magnum XL 200 at Cedar Point.

Improvements to the suspended coaster ride resulted in orders from the amusement park owners with the Big Bad Wolf built at Busch Gardens, Williamsburg in 1984; Iron Dragon at Cedar Point in 1987; XLR-8 at Astroworld in 1984, and Ninja at Six Flags Magic Mountain in 1988.

Toomer led Arrow on to design a series of jumbo multi-inversion coasters, with several loops, a boomerang section, and 360-degree helix turns, delivering plenty of air time or negative g . The twisting ribbon of metal track, held in a cradle of steel columns, coiled and double backed on itself for over a mile, creating a new thrill for coaster fans. It was an extension of the Schwarzkopf looping coasters.

Steel appeal was now the fashion; the woodies were becoming yesterday's news and every park owner wanted a steel ride. First on the scene was the Loch Ness Monster at Busch Gardens, Williamsburg, in 1978, followed by the Vortex at Kings Island, which climbs 148 feet to spin riders upside-down six times, totally disorienting them through the two and a half minute ride. Then there was the red menace, the Viper, built in 1990 at Six Flags Magic Mountain, with the longest drop of 171 feet and which included sixteen changes in elevation.

Competition was hotting up, new rides had to be developed at regular intervals to keep ahead of the other manufacturers in the field. There was big money to be earned in the amusement park industry and Arrow needed to maintain their turnover. So Toomer added the classic hypercoaster range to the Arrow stock to match the wooden monsters of Summers and Dinn that were capturing market share. The hyper coaster was an out and back gravity ride with no inversions, and designed just like the great wooden rides, except it was built to run on tubular steel track, with neoprene wheels and fiberglass car bodies. The breathtaking height that these coasters scaled beat the standing record for speed and first drop plunge. For example, the record-breaking Desperado at Buffalo Bill's Casino Resort, Nevada, which was built in 1994 in one of the most stunning settings for a roller coaster.

Toomer still hopes that one day the Pipeline Coaster, whose track configuration resembles a DNA molecule, will be built commercially. It is a continuously spiraling car, with the rider being spun in an Archimedes' screw motion, as the car speeds along the track. Will there be anyone man enough to ride it?

▲ The Pipeline coaster track resembles a DNA molecule chain. The prototype built by Arrow at their Utah works has never gone into commercial production.

▲ "Iron Dragon" suspended coaster at Cedar Point, Ohio.

▲ Gemini was one of only two steel-track, wooden racing coasters designed by Arrow.

▶ The compact and portable, vertical reverse point, shuttle looper, Weiner Looping, built in 1982.

ANTON SCHWARZKOPF (1924—)

Schwarzkopf, the "superdooperlooper man" was a carpenter by training. He is a big hearted yet reclusive man, of stout build, and with a soft smile, who transferred his talent from carpentry to manufacturing roller coasters and amusement park rides when approaching the ripe old age of forty. At times the tubular masts and struts that hold up a Schwarzkopf coaster ride seem so wafer thin and transparent to the eye that it appears incomprehensible, just like a row of pencils would appear if they were holding up a bridge! Anton Schwarzkopf has a genius for designing lightweight steel structures to resist the dynamic forces generated by an accelerating toboggan, with the greatest economy of effort.

His structures can be made transportable or static in their assembly and final position, squeezing the track onto a postage stamp or rolling it out over lakes and trees according to the space available. His roller coaster structures were price competitive, extremely attractive to look at, and fashionable because they had real speed and steel appeal. In the late 80s his company employed 250 workers and owned an assembly plant covering twenty-five acres in Munsterhausen in southern Germany.

If you were to ask serious roller coaster enthusiasts today about their favorite ride, they will tell you that Schwarzkopf is the designer of two of the greatest steel roller coaster rides ever built—the Thriller, a transportable roller coaster that can be packed into fifteen truck loads and carted to any site in Europe, and Mindbender, a triple looping

▲ The shuttle looping Greezed Lightnin' at AstroWorld, Houston, designed by Schwarzkopf, 1978.

▼ Anton Schwarzkopf—"superdooperlooper" man.

▶ The minimalist steel design of a Schwarzkopf coaster, Scorpion, at Busch Gardens, Tampa.

▲ Dreier Looping, a triple-looping, portable steel coaster, built for Herr Barth, at Duren Fair, 1985.

indoor coaster built inside a giant shopping mall in Edmonton, Canada, and delivering big g's and pulverizing excitement. He has designed and built sixteen portable roller coasters—mainly for the German and Austrian leisure industry and traveling fairs—and at least fifteen static roller coasters, mainly for the American market. Over the years he has collaborated with other amusement ride manufacturers such as Intamin and Zierer. He now works exclusively for BHS in Germany and in recent years has been commissioned to design coasters for Japan, Canada, and Sweden. His son, Wieland, operates his own amusement ride and park services company very much like his father did some years ago.

Schwarzkopf is a living legend of the roller coaster or "Herr Achterbahn" (Mr. Roller Coaster) as he has been affectionately nicknamed by his associates and the amusement park industry. He built with safety and rider comfort in mind, and believed that safety of the passenger had to be of the highest standards. He incorporated the climbing radius friction drive with antilock protection. He deployed modern structural engineering methods in all his designs, fabricating the continuous track from tubular steel which he stiffened with a central box girder beam so that it did not twist or sag out of shape carrying the toboggan at high speed. The rigidity and strength of the rail section and box girder beam were sufficiently robust to support its own weight and absorb the forces from the toboggan in a spiral loop, without any additional structure. It made his roller coasters look sleek, ribbon thin, and frighteningly minimal.

A landmark year for the roller coaster innovation was 1976, when Anton Schwarzkopf designed the Looping Racer at Magic Mountain, California, at the age of fifty-two. The coaster features a circuit track that was 90 feet high with a 360-degree vertical loop, with the track snaking back on itself to pass through the center of the first vertical loop on the approach to the finish.

From here he went on to design the Superdooperlooper Racer at Hershey Park, with even more loops and spirals, with the passengers hanging upside-down for almost as long as they were upright. The single looper begat the double, the double begat the triple looper, and the triple culminated in the searing quadruple loops and breathless g forces of Thriller, built in 1986 for Herr Bruch in Andernach, West Germany. Then there was the Olympia Looper, with five loops.

Sadly in 1987 Schwarzkopf's roller coaster business went into receivership and was taken over by Intamin AG, who retained him as principal designer for many more years. He was a perfectionist, who fiddled and fine tuned a design to the very limit, causing his sponsors and accountants to despair about the extra cost and delays such last-minute changes required. He was oblivious to it all, immersed in the mechanics and ultimate smoothness of the ride. He may not have been good at calling in his debts nor getting paid for work on time, but his designs are without parallel.

▲ The five-inversion Olympic Looping by night, seen here at the Oktoberfest in Munich.

▼ "It's all got to come down:" dismantling Thriller after the Hamburg Domfest in 1989.

HOW A ROLLER COASTER WORKS: THE ANATOMY OF THE RIDE

What is so exhilarating about a roller coaster ride? Why has it become so successful and such an important attraction of the modern amusement park? What makes a great ride? Is it the speed, the first drop height, the monstrous loops and twists of steel or mountains of wood that frame the ride, air time, the danger and savagery that the ride conveys, or the sound of screaming wheels and rattling timbers? What hits the senses as you walk

through the turnstiles is the distant outline of the biggest and tallest ride in the park, an irresistible image which your eyes are drawn to like a magnet. It's the big ride that sets the pulses racing and the adrenaline flowing, and people all react quite differently as they approach them.

It gets worse when you finally sit down in the car, the horn goes, and the chain engages, giving a little jolt to the cars as it starts hauling you slowly up the terrifying incline. Your stomach starts moving to your mouth as you reach the point of no return. At the crest of the climb you look straight down a deep plunge ... the eyes see it ... the brain registers it ... but nothing prepares you for the sensation of traveling at high speed straight at the ground. The air whistles past your face ... your hands grip tightly to the handlebars, you begin to scream, your stomach has jumped out of your mouth ... thundering down the slope and then up another a force is trying to lift you right out of your seat. More hills, more dips, more stomach churning ... the brain can't take it all in, the nervous energy building up in your body must be released, so you scream and scream until it's over. You get out of the car with tingling hands, a trembling body, and streaming eyes ... and do it all over again!

The ride experience of a wooden roller coaster and steel coaster are quite different. Many coaster enthusiasts would swear that the woodies are the best, and equally as many are convinced that steel rides are even better. Steel construction has introduced higher and faster rides, with new fail-safe devices, computerized controls, and servo braking, but the basic physics of the ride has changed remarkably little since the Mauch Chunk and Thompson Scenic Railway.

There are not as many variations in wooden ride construction as there are in steel, except in the configuration of the track layout. Having said that, no two coasters will give the same ride experience, nor will two people taking the same ride experience the same thrills. What's more just because a coaster track is big and fearsome doesn't mean it packs the biggest thrill. I rate one of the smallest and deceptively tame looking rides at Blackpool Pleasure Beach, the Wild Mouse, as more terrifying than riding the fastest and meanest looking steel coaster in Europe, the Pepsi Max Big One.

▲ "Plunging down the first drop with your stomach in your mouth ..."

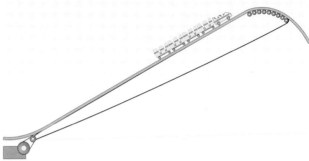

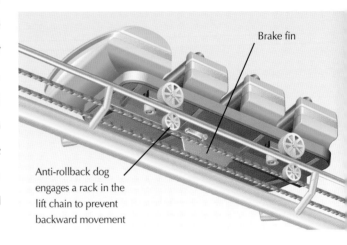

At the top of a slope, a stationary roller coaster train (1) has energy. This energy, called potential gravitational energy, can be used to move downhill at speed. Once the train starts moving down the slope (2), this turns into the kinetic energy of motion, which carries the train to the top of the next slope (3). There it changes back to potential energy. The top of each slope has to be slightly lower than the one before it because the train loses some of its energy to friction against the track and to air resistance.

How a Ride Works

At the starting station the train attaches itself to a moving chain that pulls it up the first steep incline—the lift hill—and on to the first drop. Devices called chain dogs are located on two or more of the cars. These engage with the moving chain like a sprocket does to a roll of film, and the train is pulled up the steep incline giving that distinctive clanking sound. At the crest of the lift hill a release mechanism on the track uncouples the chain dogs as the car passes over, allowing the train to speed down the slope by the force of its own weight.

At the top of the first drop and any other drop, a roller coaster has climbed high above the ground and possesses stored energy or potential energy. This energy is converted to the energy of motion or kinetic energy as the train travels down the slope and up the other side to the top of the next drop, where it is converted back to potential energy and so on. The tops of successive slopes have got to be slightly lower than the one before, because the train looses some of its kinetic energy to friction against the track and wheel bearings, and to air resistance. This is the basics of the law of conservation of energy on which all gravity rides work on. Of course there is a little more to it than that. There are centrifugal forces on the curved and inverted sections of the track, the friction loss between the wheel and the rail, the temperature of the wheel bearings, and the air flow around the cars.

▲ The climb to the top of the lift hill: (1) motor and pulley (2) chain dog pulls the car (3) chain dog is released at the top.

Brake fin

Anti-rollback dog engages a rack in the lift chain to prevent backward movement

▲ During the uphill climb, the train attaches to a moving chain that pulls it up the first steep incline. The anti-rollback dog prevents backward movement.

How Much g Force?

The exhilaration of a ride is derived from g force. Where to increase g force—the downward pressure on the body—and where to create negative g force to give the sensation of weightlessness is what makes for a good ride. Fans will wait for hours just for a minute of intense physical and emotional release.

To make a ride safe yet exciting, it is critical to keep the acceleration of the car at the bottom of the down slope to below 4 g, and to limit the negative g to 0.5 g as the car crests the top of the curve or loops upside-down. Any higher or lower g will make the body undergo too much stress. At 6 g people can start to black out and at 10 g it can kill. The smooth transition from the down slope to an upward curve is critical in good ride design, as the body is pushed through 4 g to 0.5 g in a matter of seconds.

Remember, at rest and under normal circumstances we experience our own body weight at 1 g. So at 4 g we experience the sensation of being four times heavier than our body weight, and under 0.5 g, the sensation is of being weightless and being lifted out of your seat. In one moment you are riding with King Kong on your shoulders, and the next you feel as light as a feather.

Safety and maintenance are major issues in the design, commissioning, and operating of a roller coaster ride today. There are stringent test and safety regulations to meet and certificates of ride worthiness to be signed off every year by independent safety consultants, who must log their reports with the Health and Safety Executive. Any lapse in standard will result in the ride being closed until the matter is put right. That is why there have been relatively few accidents on roller coasters.

THE DYNAMICS OF THE THRILL FACTOR—A FICTIONAL CONVERSATION WITH SCHWARZKOPF

(With reference to an article by Professor Alfred Clarke of Rochester University, New York, that appeared in RollerCoaster *magazine in 1989.)*

Bennett Why do people spend a lot of their money and time to take a roller coaster ride, which lasts for just a few moments?

Schwarzkopf Psychologists will tell you that it's the sensation of speed which triggers chemicals in the brain to give feelings of intense excitement during the ride and calm when the ride is over. Certain endorphins are released by the brain to stimulate the heart and quicken the pulse to 160 beats per minute. The release and calm experienced at the end of the ride is close to the sensation of an orgasm. We scream, yell, bellow, cry, and holler to let every last ounce of tension go. For many this outburst is an important catharsis.

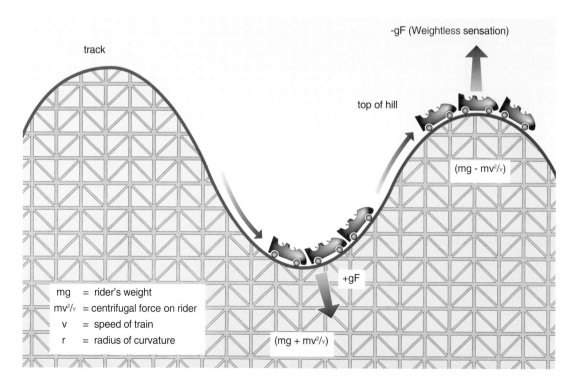

-gF (Weightless sensation)

track

top of hill

$(mg - mv^2/r)$

+gF

mg	= rider's weight
mv^2/r	= centrifugal force on rider
v	= speed of train
r	= radius of curvature

$(mg + mv^2/r)$

▶ The g force experienced at the bottom and top of a hill.

Some roller coaster fanatics claim to sleep better after a long day of screaming. It's their primal scream therapy at sixty miles an hour, and it keeps them sane.

Bennett But the key question is how are these dynamic forces exerted on the body and what stops the rider from falling out of the toboggan?

Schwarzkopf Now we need to get technical and refer to the equation of dynamic equilibrium: $S = mg + \text{or} - m(a_c + a_{pc})$

S is the seat force, which is the total force exerted on the passenger by the coaster through contact with the seat, and mg is the gravity force of the passenger's own weight, and does not change. The inertia force exerted by the coaster to the passenger due to the acceleration is given by $m(a_c + a_{pc})$ where m is the mass of the passenger and a_c is the acceleration of the toboggan and a_{pc} is the acceleration of the passenger relative to the toboggan. Actually a_{pc} is usually ignored because you don't get thrown about too much in a toboggan, if you are properly strapped in.

S is the force the passenger will experience. So when the coaster has stopped ma_c is zero and the passenger will naturally experience the reaction of his own weight from the seat.

If however ma_c is negative and $mg = -ma_c$, then S becomes zero and the passenger will experience weightlessness for a short time. As ma_c gets positive, S becomes larger, and the passenger starts to feel a greater force in the seat.

Bennett The most immediate way to produce acceleration and an increase or decrease in the g force is surely to run the toboggan over a vertically curved track.

Schwarzkopf Yes, and the sharper or tighter the radius, the greater is the g force experienced. The centrifugal acceleration due to a toboggan on a curved track is given by the equation v^2/r, where v^2 is the speed of the coaster and r is the radius of curvature.

We have a simplified equilibrium equation for a vertically curved track of constant radius where:

$S = m(g + \text{or} - v^2/r)$

So if $v^2/r = g$, the passenger experiences weightlessness, provided the centrifugal force is opposing the gravity force and has a negative value.

Weightlessness in the seat will only occur towards the crest of a vertical curve, where the upward centrifugal force is directly opposite to the downward gravity force of the passenger's weight.

If the coaster was traveling along the bottom arc of the curve, then the centrifugal force will act in the same direction as the gravity force, and has a positive value to increase the downward force.

Bennett There is another condition that appeals to most roller coaster riders and that

▲ The Revolution at Six Flags Magic Mountain, California.

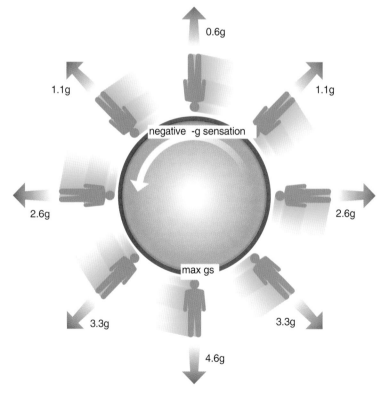

0.6g

1.1g   1.1g

negative -g sensation

2.6g   2.6g

max gs

3.3g   3.3g

4.6g

▲ The g force along a corkscrew loop.

is being hurled at 60 m.p.h. upside-down, without falling out! It would be reassuring to know what happens in the dynamics of the looping coaster rides.

Schwarzkopf Consider a looping coaster with a circle radius r and traveling at a speed of vt over the top of the crest, then the force S_t at the top of the loop is:

$S_t = m(g - v_t^2/r)$

The gravity force g and the centrifugal force V_t^2/r are in opposite directions. The speed of the coaster and track is designed to ensure that over the top section the centrifugal force is greater than the gravity force. This ensures that there is a net upward force keeping the passenger in the seat, as the toboggan travels upside-down. All toboggans have shoulder harnesses, so that even if a wheel bearing fails and the speed drops below the critical value the passenger will not fall out.

To determine the toboggan speed required at the top of the loop, say we set the seat force S_t equal to a quarter of normal weight, while the riders are upside-down:

$S_t = 0.25 \, mg = m(g - v_t^2/r)$, where $r = H/2$, thus $v_t^2 = 3 \, gH/8$

If H, the diameter of the curve is 60 feet, then $v_t = 27$ ft/sec or 19 m.p.h., a modest speed.

However the difficult problem now arises, as the toboggan and passengers travel down to the bottom of the loop. We calculate the speed at the bottom of the loop using the conservation of energy equation:

$v_b^2 = v_t^2 + 2 \, gH$, where the kinetic energy at the bottom of the ride must equal the potential energy and kinetic energy at the top of the ride. By working with this and the dynamic equilibrium equation we find that:

$S_b = 6 \, mg - S_t$

In other words there is a force of 5.75 mg at the bottom of the curve, with the passenger experiencing 5.75 g. This is too great for the comfort of the passengers. We also know that the force at the top is only 0.25 g. We must therefore increase the g force at the top to 0.5 g and somehow reduce the toboggan speed at the bottom to reduce the g force to 4 g, for rider comfort.

Bennett How then do we design the looping track to keep the ride fast, yet safe through the loop and also control the g forces?

Schwarzkopf We must change the curvature at the bottom of the loop to flatten the

Rear seats travel faster during plunges; more of the total ride time is spent at fast downward speeds.

Riders in the train experience acceleration as they are pulled over the crest of a hill

The shorter the train, or the higher the drop, the less difference there is in riding the front or the back of the train.

Front seats travel fastest during uphill swings.

▲ Making the most of the ride on a nonlooping coaster.

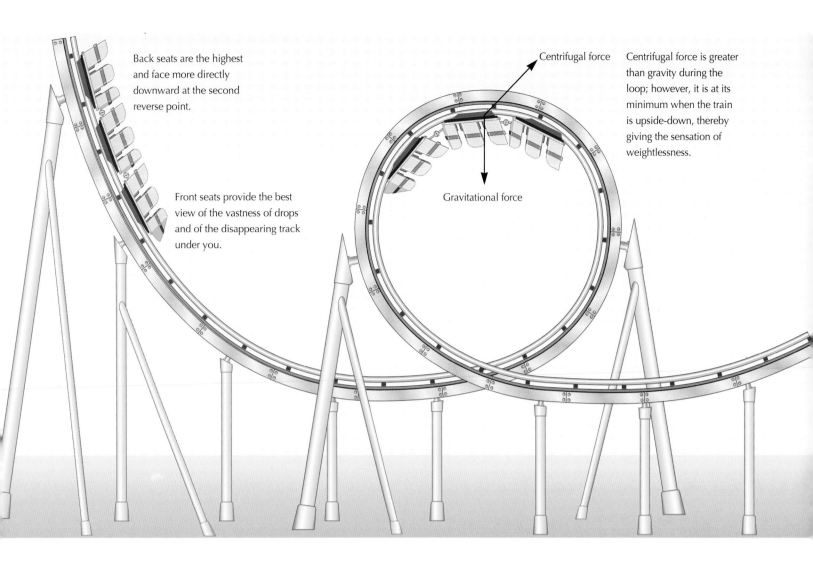

Back seats are the highest and face more directly downward at the second reverse point.

Front seats provide the best view of the vastness of drops and of the disappearing track under you.

Centrifugal force

Centrifugal force is greater than gravity during the loop; however, it is at its minimum when the train is upside-down, thereby giving the sensation of weightlessness.

Gravitational force

▲ Making the most of the ride on a looping coaster.

radius to reduce the centrifugal force, without losing train speed. The radius of curvature of looping and corkscrew coasters will continuously change as the toboggan descends and this is called a clothoid configuration. This keeps the centrifugal force within reasonable bounds and the ride reasonably comfortable.

WHERE SHOULD YOU SIT ON A RIDE?

Before discussing the differences between wooden and steel coasters, stand-up and suspended coasters, looping and shuttle coasters, jumbo jets and wild mouse, let's consider the ride experience of sitting at the front or back of the train.

The rear seats of any train travel slightly faster than the front seats because more of the weight of the train is accelerating down the slope. Riders in the rear seat will experience more negative g or air time as the rear car whips over the top of the crest or when they are upside-down at the top of the spiral of a looping coaster. Many riders prefer the back seat because you can see the rest of the train going upside-down in front of you.

The greater the height of the drop and smaller the radius curvature, the more intense is the ride. For those in the front of the train, the ride is a lot smoother and there is a clear view of the track ahead. The shorter the train and the higher the drop, the less the difference between riding in the front or in the back.

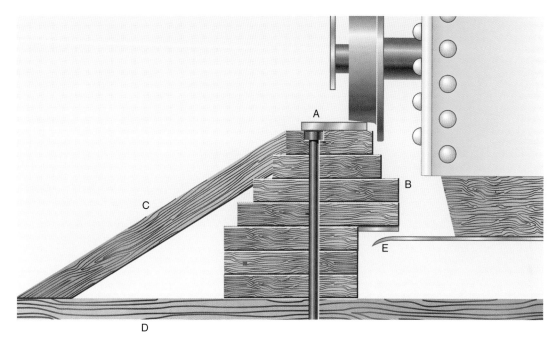

▲ Diagram illustrating the construction of the wooden track, showing the flanged wheel of a Traver coaster car: (A) flat steel track screwed into the running track (B) laminated wood running track (C) diagonal strut to brace the track against horizontal movement (D) timber beam supporting the running track (E) under-friction safety bar.

To enhance the ride experience, designers will introduce features and novelty to the ride. For example, the chain lift is deliberately slowed down to increase the climb duration and give the illusion of greater height in order to build up the anticipation. Those in the front cars will feel it more intensely. The loss of speed on parts of the track are compensated by incorporating curved or banked sections to enhance the sensation of speed. The close proximity of the uprights of the support structure, overhead track, and cross members dramatize the experience of speed.

Tunnels, dark sections, and riding at night tend to distort time and make the riders believe they are traveling at great speed. Lights spaced at different intervals along the track, closer over the slower section, will hide any loss in speed. Building the track out over a lake, or in a gorge, or up and over trees, or interweaving through another ride adds drama as well. This all comes into play when a new ride is being developed.

WOODEN WONDERS

The Wooden Roller Coaster

A roller coaster listed under this heading may have its support framework or superstructure built of timber or steel. Traver's later designs used steel superstructures, as did John Allen and Curtis Summers on occasion to reduce material cost and construction time. It is the track that defines a wooden roller coaster and not the superstructure. The train runs on a flat metal strip—the rail—usually 4–6 inches wide, which is secured by countersunk bolts to a laminated timber running track and cross beam supports. In the Traver and Miller days, the flat metal strip was usually 2–3 inches wide.

The laminated running track of the wooden roller coaster is made up of six to eight layers of timber, usually southern yellow pine, with each layer 2 inches thick and about 6 inches wide. In the early years when long leaf yellow pine was available it was preferred because of its strength and the lengths that could be cut. The laminated track is braced

▲ Timber "bents" being craned into position during construction of Tonnerre de Zeus at Parc Asterix, Paris, France.

by diagonal struts bolted to the cross beam supports, to keep the running track rigid, and to resist any horizontal movement from the train wheels. The flat metal under friction rail is bolted to the underside of the laminated running track. The wooden running track cushions the slams and jarring thumps of the wheels on the metal strip, to give that distinctive creaking, rattling noise of a wooden roller coaster. (Some modern coasters utilize side friction wheels to lock the train to the track, instead of the under friction wheels, with a flat metal rail fixed to the vertical face of the running track.)

The coasters of Church and Traver used flanged wheels, like those of conventional trains, to act as weight bearing and guide wheels, with either under friction wheels or steel plate to prevent the cars from jumping off the track. Miller, on the other hand, used an unflanged weight bearing wheels to run on the top rail, with side friction wheels to guide the train on the track and under friction wheels to prevent it lifting off the track. Allen and Summers designed their wooden tracks very much to the Miller specification.

The running track and supporting cross beams are carried on the superstructure which is a scaffold of braced posts called "bents" made of timber or steel. A bent is a two-dimensional frame which is self-supporting only when it is braced by a series of diagonal ties called chords. It has two legs, which are placed at right angles to the track, and a top beam forming a goal post which carries the running track. Each leg of the bent is supported on a concrete foundation dug into the ground. The bents are prefabricated

▲ The metal rail, laminated wooden track, and timber support structure of Colossus at Six Flags Magic Mountain.

▼ Repairing the track of a Scenic Railway.

▲ Wooden framed cars of early Scenic Railway coasters.

▲ The bull-nose fronts and the shorter lengths of wooden coaster cars of today. The Thunderbolt at Kennywood Park.

▼ The wonderful twisting symmetry of White Cyclone at Nagashimi Spaland, Nagoya, Japan.

▶ Looking down the first drop of an out-and-back wooden coaster, the Hoosier Hurricane at Indiana Beach, Montebello.

from 6 x 6-inch pressurized timber sections or tubular or rectangular steel hollow section. They are braced longitudinally to the adjacent bent at regular intervals along their length, as well as internally by diagonal chords, to maintain a stable and rigid construction that mirrors the contours of the track. Both the superstructure and the running track are painted to preserve and protect the timber from moisture ingress and insect infestation.

The American Eagle, designed by Curtis Summers for Intamin AG in 1981 at Six Flags Great America, Gurnee, Illinois, has a track length of 4,650 feet which required the following material in its construction.

• 2,000 concrete foundations each 2 feet in diameter and 5 feet in depth

• 1,600,000 feet of timber

• 60,720 bolts

• 30,600 pounds of nails

• 9,000 gallons of paint

To complete the ride, we need the cars to carry the passengers over the undulating track. The old wooden coaster cars had their frames and body paneling made of wood, which was strong, pliable, and easily fabricated. The frame was attached to the steel axles and wheels. Later the paneling was replaced by sheet metal, which changed to aluminum in the 60s, and then fiberglass molded to a steel chassis in the 70s. In the early years, rigid four-seater cars were coupled together in groups of up to six, with each car having two axles and two pairs of wheels. Church modified the cars to have only one axle and one pair of wheels, with each car coupled to the car ahead by a ball and socket joint, giving the cars greater articulation and three points of suspension. The two-wheeled, two-seater cars of Church's were attached to a pilot car in the front which incorporated four wheels.

Traver changed the single-axle, two-seater cars to four-seater ones, with up to five cars making up a coaster train—plus a four-wheeled pilot car—to reduce the maintenance and manufacturing costs. This configuration has been retained today except that the car bodies are built of aluminum or fiberglass molded to a steel chassis.

The majority of wooden coaster trains are a series of squat, brightly painted cars, with a blunt leading nose, making them appear like a high-speed caterpillar running along the tracks. The exception to this is the magnificent Art Deco chrome of the coaster cars built by National Amusement Devices for Forest Park in the 1940s, which now languish in the Smithsonian Museum.

Twisters, Out and Back, and Racers

There are basically two configurations of wooden track layouts: a twisting and spiraling layout on a compact site, and an out and back ribbon layout covering a large area. A

variation on the out and back is the racer, with two parallel tracks which allows two trains to race against each other. Twisters are multilayered concentric tracks that travel under, around, and over themselves. Out and backs are noticeable for their straight lengths of hills and dips with few turns, making for a faster ride than the twister which has to rely on surprise and the sensation of speed. Many rides will combine both features to give the best possible wooden coaster experience.

A wooden coaster whose first drop height is not greater than 40 feet is called a Junior Woody, while one whose highest point is less than 26 feet is called a Kiddie Coaster. But no matter what the size or type of wooden coaster, they all have one thing in common: they shake, they rattle, and they roll, as the train thunders over the cushioning and pliant laminations of wood running track.

And just because there are not as many wooden coaster types as there are steel rides, it does not mean that woodies are predictable and stereotyped ... far from it.

STEEL APPEAL

Tubular Steel Track Coasters

It's the tubular steel track that distinguishes the steel coaster from the wooden coaster in both coaster technology and ride experience. Usually the whole structure—the track and superstructure—is prefabricated from tubular steel and box girder sections. The track is elevated on slender steel supports, the bases of which are only a little wider than the tracks themselves. As a result, once aboard the train, the riders cannot see the structure beneath them. An exception is the Gemini in Cedar Point and the Ultimate at Lightwater Valley, which have wooden support structures and look just like classic wooden coasters. Quite a few mine trains are built with a wooden support structure.

Steel coaster structures appear minimal, lightweight, and almost transparent in daylight. They are characterized by their brightly painted colors, tall yet slender vertical supports, ribbonlike track, and streamlined, aerodynamic shape of the leading car.

In the construction of the Pepsi Max Big One, Europe's tallest, at 235 feet, and fastest roller coaster, at 80 m.p.h., the following materials were used:

- 2,215 tons of steel, which laid end to end would reach 40 miles
- 60,000 bolts
- 237 steel stanchions and 94 steel monopods to support the track
- The surface area of painted steel is 42,000 square yards, the equivalent of 6 soccer pitches
- 1,270 piles were driven to form the foundation for the steel superstructure

The tubular steel rail of a steel coaster gives an extremely smooth ride, with none of the side to side jostling of a wooden coaster. This is largely due to better profiling of the

▲ The almost transparent supports of Magnum XL 200.

▼ The tubular steel track and wheel arrangement of a steel coaster car.

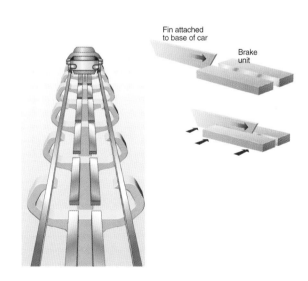

▲ The computer-operated brake fin of a steel track roller coaster car.

◄ Some people prefer the steel appeal of a multi-inversion coaster such as Kumba at Busch Gardens, Tampa.

steel track and the sets of polyurethane-coated wheels that keep the steel coaster clamped to the track. The weight-bearing wheels of the cars are typically made from layers of polyurethane bonded to the wheel hub, but these are sometimes changed to nylon wheels for winter running because they are harder. Smaller under friction wheels run below the weight-bearing ones and operate when there is negative g, to prevent the train lifting off the track. Even smaller side friction wheels come into play to prevent the train from sliding as it goes around a horizontal turn. The steel coaster does not make the clanking, rattling roar of a wooden coaster. It's more the whoosh of rushing air and hiss of sizzling wheels, as it thunders overhead.

Steel coaster cars are molded from glass fiber bodies mounted on a steel chassis. The cars are fitted with brake fins that slot loosely between brake blocks fitted at particular places along the track circuit, and at the station. When the brakes are activated by computer sensors on the track, the moving part of the brake block clamps onto the brake fin to slow the train or to halt it.

Steel coasters are generally divided into nonlooping and looping or inversion rides, either of which can run on a complete circuit layout or a shuttle circuit layout where a train travels back and forth on the same track. They can be designed to run with the passengers sitting upright, or suspended below the track, or standing up in a harness, hence the name suspended and stand up coasters. They can be categorized in the following way:

Corkscrew

Trains of twenty-four passengers, who are sitting in the conventional upright position, and are well secured by deepset seat belts and over-the-shoulder restraints before they are carried up a 70-foot chain lift to be released, down and up through two barrel-type rolls, hence the corkscrew name. After a 180-degree turn, the coaster heads down to the station.

Invented by Arrow Developments in 1975, the uniqueness of this ride and the minimal space it needs for construction have made the corkscrew one of the most popular of the steel rides.

Vertical Looping Coaster

These are the more severe of the circuit looping rides, characterized by a high chain lift, fast turns, and deep dips very much like a wooden coaster except that along the way the train is inverted by one or more stomach-wrenching vertical loops.

The vertical looping coaster was pioneered by Anton Schwarzkopf and Intamin. They

▼ A typical Corkscrew steel coaster. This one is at Geuga Lake, Ohio.

▲ A vertical-looping steel coaster, the Laser at Dorney Park.

were designed to be fast rides, delivering plenty of g force and out of the seat feeling. Their design and structural layouts, standing out like sign writing on the sky, can frequently be picked up from a long way away. Portable versions of the looping coaster were developed by Schwarzkopf for many of Germany's traveling fairs.

Shuttle Looping Coaster (Horizontal Reverse Point)

The train is catapulted out of the station, like a rocket, 40 feet up to the first drop. Over the top and down the dips and then up a vertical loop at 45 m.p.h., when passengers experience 3 g. Just as quickly, it spirals out of the 30-foot helix giving riders a moment of negative g as they hang upside-down. After the loop is completed, the train goes up a hill, then levels off, and stops for a moment until it is catapulted backward through the loop and to the boarding station. The short ride duration of under one minute is packed with excitement on a very cramped site and was a great success for Arrow in the 80s.

▼ The catapult launch of a boomerang shuttle looping coaster. The Cobra at the West Midlands Safari Park, England.

Shuttle Looping Coaster (Vertical Reverse Point)

Even more dramatic than the horizontal reverse point (HRP) shuttle looper is the vertical reverse point (VRP) looper, developed by Anton Schwarzkopf, giving the most intense coaster ride ever conceived. The loading platform is nearer the ground than the HRP. The catapult mechanism shoots the train at the vertical loop at 55 m.p.h., which hits the bottom of the down slope at over 4 g for an instant. After the loop, which stands at 61 feet,

▲ The boomerang section of Cobra.

the train is carried by momentum up a cut-off hill, 140 feet high and raked at a 70-degree angle. A weightless moment occurs before the train reverses back down the steep slope, hurtles through the loop, speeds through the boarding station, to brake part way up a second near vertical incline. The riders now face forward one last time as the train runs back down the slope to the station to stop.

Boomerang Shuttle Looping Coaster

A later variation on the VRP designed by Vekoma, a Dutch-based ride manufacturer, increased the ride duration by adding a central boomerang section and a looping element along one leg of the horseshoe layout. Two raking inclines at each end of the horseshoe act as the start and reverse points of the ride. The train is pulled backward up the first 125-foot incline, then released to travel through the station, through the boomerang or open helix section, the vertical loop, and up the other incline before reversing backward through the loop and boomerang. The boomerang's compact structure and many inversions have made it the world's most popular production steel coaster, with twenty-five exact copies built to date.

▲ Bolliger and Mabillard's Batman—The Ride at Six Flags Over Mid-America, an inverted looping coaster.

▲ A suspended nonlooping coaster, AirRace, at Bobbejaanland, Belgium.

▶ Close-up of the steel track, suspended coaster car, and wheel arrangement of AirRace.

Suspended Coaster

The trains are suspended below the tubular steel track as individual gondolas, that can swing from side to side at angles of up to 45 degrees to the horizontal as they bank around the turns and twists. The coaster was first developed by Arrow as a non-looping ride, running on a continuous circuit with a top speed of 56 m.p.h. It was marketed as the ride that came closest to free flight and first appeared at Kings Island, Ohio, in 1981 and was called the Bat. Vekoma later modified the suspended gondolas to be more like ski-lift seats that did not swing, to enable them to loop, to be inverted, and to rotate with the twist of the tubular track. They built a number of these thrilling rides for parks in North America, culminating in the phenomenal red devil, the Great Nor'Easter built at Moreys Pier, Wildwood, in 1995.

The Swiss firm of Bolliger and Mabillard (B & M) refined the suspended coaster track and gondola design in the 90s, allowing four people to ride in a rigid row of suspended seats, where previously they were only two, increasing the revenue earnings per ride. The rigid structure of the suspended seat allows the coaster to invert and loop which was not possible with a swinging gondola. Through their flawless construction, innovative concepts, heart line spins, and state of the art technology, B & M have become one of the most sought after steel coaster designers in the world today. The Raptor, built in

1994 at Cedar Point, is typical of a B & M design comprising slender trunks of tubular steel columns and box girder sections, supporting a lattice of twisted and coiled length of rail track. This spectacular outside looping coaster with its many loops and helix turns had the first cobra roll, where riders are turned upside-down twice as they go through it. They also designed the first inverted suspended coaster in 1992, the sensational Batman The Ride at Six Flags Great America, Illinois, where riders are inverted through loops and boomerangs.

Stand Up Coaster

In 1982, Kazou Yamada of TOGO coaster builders in Japan conceived of the kamikaze stand up roller coaster. After building a few in Japan, the stand up was exported to the U.S. and made its debut at Kings Island in 1984. The riders are secured into cleverly designed vertical supports attached to the cars, and harnessed to it in the standing position. The looping track layout hurls the standing riders down the dips, through a loop and horizontal helix turns, before returning to the station. The sensation of speed and sheer terror as the riders fall head first down the drops and through the loop makes this ride quite an awesome challenge. It does not need to be fast to be frightening.

Hyper Coaster

To respond to the success of the mega wooden coasters of Allen and Summers, Arrow developed the hyper steel coaster concept. It was modeled on the classic out and back wooden coaster rides except they were made taller, longer, and faster because they were built in steel. The Magnum XL 200 made its debut in 1989 at Cedar Point and was the first full circuit coaster to break the 200-foot height plateau and to achieve a speed in excess of 70 m.p.h. It was voted by coaster fans as one of the best steel coasters in the world. The record was broken when Arrow built their third hyper coaster, the Pepsi Max Big One, at Blackpool Pleasure Beach, and later in 1994 with the fabulously esthetic Desperado at Buffalo Bill's Resort. The Desperado, along with Steel Phantom at Kennywood Park, has the longest drop of 225 feet and a top speed approaching 80 m.p.h. The tallest hyper coaster ride today is Fujiyama at Hijukyo Highlands Park in Japan.

Mine Trains

The boxlike cars of the mine train are designed to resemble coal mine wagons and are reminiscent of some early coasters which were actual mine cars. The continuous circuit is smaller than a conventional wooden coaster track, and, using less material, they were

▲ Stand-up steel coaster King Cobra, at Paramount's Kings Island.

◀ Steel hyper coaster, Magnum XL 200, situated at Cedar Point.

cheap to build, but fun to ride. They usually had a scenic or cavern backdrop, a short chain lift of no more than 50 feet and gave the rider the precarious sensation of toppling over as they dipped through the tunnels and tight turns on their narrow rails. They were developed by Arrow in the 60s and are smooth, tummy tingling, non-violent, family oriented rides.

Jet Stars, Jumbo Jets, and Wild Mouse

There were many small steel coaster rides built after the Second World War. They were very compact and were made to fit confined sites, typically the seaside pier. Many were portable in construction and were very popular in Europe. They were designed with single cars or just two or three cars running on tight, twisting, continuously spiraling track. Two of the best white knuckle rides were the Jumbo Jets, designed by Anton Schwarzkopf, and the Wild Mouse, first developed by Carl Miler in 1957. The Wild Mouse ride was devised when there was a shortage of building materials in the industry.

The Jumbo Jets and Jet Stars were built on a bigger track layout, and have electric-powered toboggan cars, which haul themselves up the ascent tower by a friction drive. Once at the top of the 50-foot helix ascent tower, the train is released down the multilayered figure-eight track, which features steep-sided turns and continuous positive g force.

THINGS TO COME

As amusement ride technology advances in the twenty-first century, we can only imagine what is to come. The definition of a roller coaster may change because of the structure and dynamics of a new ride. There are many rides today that some would say are an

▲ Mine train, Goldrusher, at Six Flags Magic Mountain.

◄ The 90 m.p.h. free fall coaster, Superman the Escape, at Six Flags Magic Mountain.

▶ The heartline spin of Toga's Ultra Twister, at Six Flags AstroWorld.

▼ New for 1998, the Power Tower at Cedar Point blasts riders up and down four 300-foot towers at 50 m.p.h., but it is not a roller coaster.

▲ Euro Mir, a new spinning ride that runs on a conventional steel roller coaster track. Designed by Mack in 1997.

extension of the roller coaster. The Free Falls built by Intamin in the 80s, is a straight up and down gravity ride, but is it a bungee jump in a train or a roller coaster? It consists of a skeletal steel elevator tower which transports four passengers to the top. Once up there, the car is moved to the outside of the tower where it hangs and then drops without warning, free wheeling down the tower along a steel track which then curves and levels out as it nears the ground. Superman The Escape, which opened in 1997 at Six Flags Magic Mountain, uses linear motors built along the track to propel a fifteen-seater coaster-type car from a standing start straight up a tower 400 feet high, reaching speeds in excess of 90 m.p.h. on the way. When it gets near to the top, it stops momentarily before plummeting backward down the tower, braking to a halt along 900 feet of level track.

Speed, height, and big g's will surely sustain the roller coaster as the supreme ride in the future. We may also see a lot more novelty rides, with the emphasis on fun rather than fear, for all the family to enjoy, like the unique Euro Mir developed by Mack in 1997. Four glass-sided silo-like towers, 92 feet high, transport a set of umbrella-shaped cars inside them to the top, where they then roll down a spiral figure-eight track. As the cars travel along the tubular steel track, they spin on their axes at precise points along it. Can this be the start of a new generation of spinning coasters and more family oriented rides? In 1995, Intamin designed a roller coaster for Lotte World in Seoul where vehicles spin like teacups along the track, caused by the turns and curves along the circuit, and governed by the weight of the passengers.

On the other hand, TOGO are developing "heartline" coasters, like the Ultra Twister and the Viper built at Six Flags Great Adventure Park, which is capable of continuous 360-degree rolls on a ringed support structure, that spin-dries you through the air. The ride is designed so that the center of the spiraling maneuver is located around the rider's heart to prevent black outs! Do the passengers have to be the same height before they can ride this blood-curdling ride so that all their hearts line up correctly, we might ask anxiously!

And as for the man who suffers from motion sickness and can't take a white knuckle ride, but designs plenty of them—Ron Toomer also hopes that his revolutionary "pipeline" coaster, with heartline spins, plenty of g, and air time, will be marketable quite soon. But he is at a loss to explain what is going to happen in the next twenty years. The kind of coaster a park wants is dictated more and more by marketing people, he suggests, not by the ride operators or designers. It comes down to "what we can market" rather than what would be the best and most exciting ride. As far as what the future holds for new rides, nothing is predictable according to Toomer.

"Twenty years ago we were talking about going upside-down. Even when this led to the Corkscrew in 1974 we could not have guessed then what we'd be doing today. There is no technical limit as to how high a coaster can be built, but someday there will be an economic cost limit. Today though, the cost of a new coaster is

▲ Mantis, a stand-up inverted roller coaster designed by Bolliger and Mabillard in 1996, for Cedar Point.

▶ The track layout of Mantis: (1) 119-foot high vertical loop (2) 103-foot high dive loop (3) 360-degree banked turn (4) 83-foot high inclined loop (5) 360-degree flat spin (6) figure-eight finish.

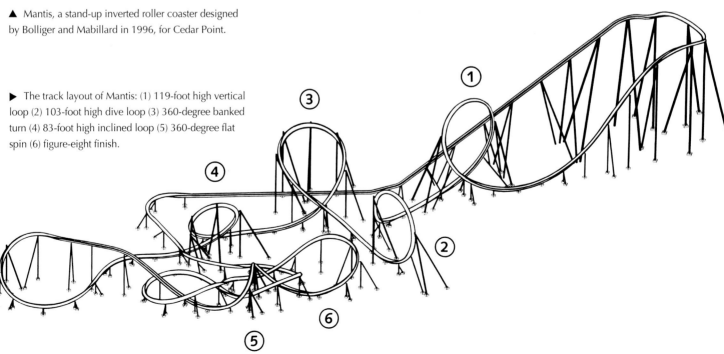

generally returned in its first year through increased attendance at the park."

Toomer believes we will surely see larger coasters being built because of the competition between amusement parks and the need to keep the public interested enough to make return visits.

Dr. John Roberts, a partner of structural engineers Allott and Lomax in England, believes that the roller coaster has already got to its limit on g-force exhilaration. By raising the height of the first drop to, say, 400 feet, a roller coaster may reach a speed of 95 m.p.h. at the bottom of the drop but, in order to keep the force on the body within safe limits, the acceleration must not be greater than 4 g. To ensure this, the bottom curve must be longer and flatter. There may be little sense in building taller, more expensive coasters if there is no benefit in the ride sensation. The Pepsi Max Big One, which he was involved with, has a greater acceleration than a supercharged high performance sports car, and reaches 60 m.p.h. from a standing start in just three seconds. And that's a coaster with no engine!

The cinematically themed rides, like Outer Limits and Space Mountain, may lead on to greater sophistication in special effects, 3D screens, and the virtual reality of a flight to Mars now that Mariner is sending back sharp images of the planet's surface. It is possible there will be a revival of the Scenic Railway of L. A. Thompson and the old-style amusement park rides, where the emphasis will be on nostalgia, fun, novelty, and family entertainment.

The possibilities are endless and the future choices unpredictable, that we can guarantee. At the time of writing, over a hundred roller coasters are being designed for parks around the world, emphatically confirming the continuing popularity of the white knuckle ride for the foreseeable future.

CHAPTER FOUR

THE GREATEST WHITE KNUCKLE RIDES
OF TODAY

This chapter is dedicated to all roller coaster fans, whether you have only just started on your discovery of thrill rides or have been coastering for many years. A select group of roller coaster enthusiasts—most of them connoisseurs of the white knuckle ride experience—has been invited from around the world to name their all-time favorite ride and to tell us what makes them so special. These people have been riding coasters for as long as they can remember and have traveled the world in search of the very best, so they ought to know. Their infectious enthusiasm and colorful explanation of their choice is nearly as expressive as the images of the great rides they have chosen.

It's interesting to note that roller coaster enthusiasts come from all walks of life, just like other sports fans of, say, baseball or soccer. In this group we have a government tax inspector, a computer game designer, a lawyer, a computer engineer, an historian and archivist, a construction engineer, a truck driver, a composer and college professor, as well as journalists, photographers, and editors of amusement park magazines.

And to remind you how varied is the choice of the people's favorite in the U.S., for example, over the years, here is a list taken from *Guide to Ride* published by ACE in 1991 following a major poll they organized amongst coaster buffs. Compare that with the NAPHA short list for best ride in 1996. When Justin Garvanovic was recently asked about the *Guide to Ride* list, he just rolled his eyes, and said "No Way." By way of explanation he added that a few years ago he rated the Beast at Kings Island one of the best wooden roller coasters, but modifications to the ride in recent years, with heavy braking on the normal high speed sections has taken the thrill away, and it's not as good any more ... but that's only his opinion.

◀ Colossus, Six Flags Magic Mountain

The *Guide to Ride: 1991* (reproduced by kind permission of ACE)
(most number of votes for a coaster as a personal favorite)

Wooden Coasters
1 Beast, Kings Island, Ohio
2 Cyclone, Astroland, Coney Island, Brooklyn, New York
3 Texas Giant, Six Flags Over Texas, Arlington
4 Timber Wolf, Worlds Of Fun, Kansas City
5 Mr. Twister, Elitch Gardens, Denver (now sadly dismantled)
6 Thunderbolt, Kennywood, West Mifflin
7 Riverside Cyclone, Riverside Park, Agawan
8 Colossus, Six Flags Magic Mountain, Valencia
9 Hercules, Dorney Park, Allentown
10 Giant Dipper, Belmont Park, San Diego

Steel Coasters
1 Magnum XL-200, Cedar Point, Sandusky
2 Mind Bender, Six Flags Over Georgia, Atlanta
3 Loch Ness Monster, Busch Gardens, Williamsburg
4 Big Bad Wolf, Busch Gardens, Williamsburg
5 Vortex, Kings Island, Ohio
6 (equal) Mindbender, Galaxyland, West Edmonton Mall, Alberta, Canada Viper, Six Flags Magic Mountain, Valencia
8 Revolution, Six Flags Magic Mountain, Valencia
9 Great American Scream Machine, Six Flags Adventure, Jackson
10 Iron Wolf, Six Flags Great Amercia, Gurnee

The 1996 NAPHA members votes for best rides were:

Favorite wooden coasters
1 Thunderbolt, Kennywood, West Mifflin, U.S.
2 Megaphobia, Oakwood, U.K.
3 Texas Giant, Six Flags Over Texas, Arlington, U.S.
4 Cyclone, Astroland, Coney Island, U.S.
5 Comet, Great Escape, Lake George, U.S.
6 Raven, Holiday World, Santa Claus, U.S.

Favorite steel rides
1 Magnum XL-200, Cedar Point, Sandusky, U.S.
2 Raptor, Cedar Point, Sandusky, U.S.
3 Nemesis, Alton Towers, Staffordshire, U.K.
4 Steel Phantom, Kennywood, West Mifflin, U.S.
5 Pepsi Max Big One, Blackpool Pleasure Beach, U.K.
6 Loch Ness Monster, Busch Gardens, Williamsburg, U.S.

THE GREATEST WHITE KNUCKLE RIDES OF TODAY

MINDBENDER
GALAXYLAND, WEST EDMONTON MALL, ALBERTA, CANADA
Randy Geisler

"I've ridden 395 different roller coasters in five different countries, written about them, spoken about them, and talked on television about them as a supposed expert on roller coasters, and served as President of the American Coaster Enthusiasts Club in my time out of love for them. As to my favorite coaster, I've often replied, when asked that question, 'it's the one I'm riding on right now!'

"I, like many coaster enthusiasts, feel the barnstorming rough and tumble of woodies are best, but there are some steel coasters capable of delivering a twisted dementia punch that woodies can't match. The Bandit in the Yomiuri Land, Tokyo, is one of them; another is Mindbender at Galaxyland within the West Edmonton Mall, which is my personal favorite for severely intense coastering *in extremis*. The 136-foot lift hill seems to scrape the Mall ceiling before the coaster plummets the equivalent of twelve stories, in a last gasp dive that twists and curves underneath itself. This is followed by nonstop severe swoops, near black out intense g force climbs, and triple loops that send riders through breathtaking astronaut-in-training maneuvers."

▲ *"The coaster plummets the equivalent of a twelve-story building."*

◀ *"The intense turns, severe loops, and big gs of Mindbender is steel coasting in extremis."* Not recommended for the faint-hearted!

◀ *"Blasting out of the lift hill …"*

Ride Statistics
Steel triple looping ride, 4,080-foot track, speed 58 m.p.h., built 1986, Schwarzkopf.

GIANT DIPPER
SANTA CRUZ BOARDWALK, SANTA CRUZ, CALIFORNIA, U.S.
Tom Maglione

"This ride is not the tallest, the fastest, or the longest, but it combines so many elements of great coasters that overall it surpasses every other ride for me. It's a classic, combining drops and peaks with good side turns and a superior turnaround over the station. Foremost among its qualities are its wooden construction and seaside location. The sight of the Giant Dipper assaults your senses as does the shoreline of Monterey Bay, and the smell of popcorn, corn dogs, burgers, and salt spray. You feel the bottom drop out from under you as you are yanked into the surprising tunnel at the beginning of the ride."

Ride Statistics
Wooden out and back twister ride, 2,640-foot track, speed 55 m.p.h., built 1924, Arthur Loeff.

▲ *"The sight of the Giant Dipper assaults your senses."*

▶ *"It's a classic because it combines so many elements of great wooden coasters."*

THE CYCLONE
ASTROLAND, CONEY ISLAND, BROOKLYN, NEW YORK, U.S.

Barry Norman

"Although the modern-day steel coaster can pack a punch, with leviathan inversions and corkscrews, and stand up and sit down combinations, they invariably make me believe that they could all have come out of the same 'crate of parts'—everything costed and nothing valued. Let's face it, all coasters these days come via the silicone mind of computer-aided design or CAD machines; it's just that the wooden coasters definitely feel as if they have a soul!

"My all-time favorite coaster will inevitably come from the roaring twenties—the Golden Age of the roller coaster. It will be the ride that I 'go on' in my mind every time I hear the dentist's drill start up. It will be the ride that reminds me of my youth and the thrill later in life of sharing the screams with my wife, Jackie. It was the ride we flew out to New York to ride fifty times on September 2, 1992, to celebrate our silver wedding anniversary. It can only be the Coney Island Cyclone for me."

◀ *"This coaster has a soul. It is the ride I 'go on' every time I hear the dentist drill start up."*

Ride Statistics

Wooden out and back twister, 2,640-foot track, speed 50 m.p.h., built 1927, Harry Baker/Vernon Keenan.

▲ Barry and Jackie Norman riding the Cyclone on their silver wedding anniversary.

◀ *"This is the ride that reminds me of my youth, every time."*

▲ "An utterly painless experience that is astonishing for its out-of-body sensations."

▶ "The theater of John Wardley's set design around Bolliger & Mabillard's Nemesis ride is mind-blowing."

NEMESIS

ALTON TOWERS, ALTON, STAFFORDSHIRE, ENGLAND

David Bennett

"The music of Graham Stuart and the theater of John Wardley's set design around Bolliger and Mabillard Nemesis ride is mind blowing. Red dye gurgles and cascades down walls and creeks into a ravine, where a huge dragon monster crouches ready for take-off for another kill. It is difficult to believe that you have actually ridden Nemesis as you watch groups of people being flung, somersaulted, and cartwheeled through the air at 50 m.p.h. My partner, Jennifer, would not let me ride it the first day; she was too scared for me! The *Jurassic Park* music that blasts over the air as the ride climbs to the first drop is terrifying.

"It was a whirlwind, light-headed ride that was smooth and fast ... an utterly painless experience that is astonishing for its variety of movement and out-of-body sensation. The vertical loop was the most timeless moment of the whole thing. A wonderful ride."

▲ *"The Jurassic Park music that blasts over the air as the ride climbs the first drop is terrifying."*

Ride Statistics

Steel suspended multi-inversion ride, 2,350-foot track, speed 50 m.p.h., built 1994, Bolliger and Mabillard.

▲ "This roller coaster is reminiscent of the great 20s' rough-and-tumble coasters."

▶ "It reminds me of my all-time favorite—the fabulous Bobs at Riverview Park."

▲ *"A ride on the Cyclone is one of controlled mayhem from start to finish."*

▶ *"The track is intense, acutely angled, with wicked turns, and severely banked corners."*

RIVERSIDE CYCLONE

RIVERSIDE PARK, AGAWAN, MASSACHUSETTS

Jim Abbate

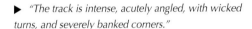

"Today, the ride that reminds me most of my all-time favorite—the fabulous Bobs at Riverview Park, designed by Church, and built by Traver, but sadly demolished in 1967—is the Cyclone at Riverside Park in Agawan, Massachusetts.

"Though it was built in 1983, this Bill Cobham designed wooden coaster is reminiscent of the great 20s 'rough and tumble' coasters. A ride on the Cyclone is one of controlled mayhem from start to finish. This coaster attacks the track like no other I know, from the intense, acutely angled first drop, through the wicked turns and severely banked corners, it's one explosive 'hell bent for leather' ride. It all happens at such a furious pace through this wall-to-wall wooden structure, that you swear when you get to the finish that you will never ride this ferocious coaster again!"

Ride Statistics

Wooden twister, 3,400-foot track, speed 60 m.p.h., built 1983, William Cobb Associates.

MEGAPHOBIA
OAKWOOD, NARBETH, WALES, U.K.
Steven Thompson

"It looks massive; it is one mass of twisted wood. The coaster is cranked up to the top of the first drop, then woossshhh! Down and sideways we go! We turn sharp left and I'm slammed into the side of my seat. Wow! The helix and criss-cross come next, as the train drives and banks all over the place, and I'm pushed from side to side in my seat. About half way we hit the first hill and negative g and air time, where you get the real sensation of weightlessness. My feet start coming out of my shoes. Back down again with terrific speed and positive g pushing me back into the seat leaving me breathless. More twists and criss-crossing, before we hit the second hill, and more tingling air time, then down and back, before the servo brakes bring the monster safely into base."

Ride Statistics

Wooden out and back twister, 3,000-foot track, speed 55 m.p.h., built 1996, Custom Coasters International.

◀ *"It looks massive, it is massive—it is one long twist of massive wood."*

▼ *"Halfway round we hit the first hill, with so much negative g that my feet start coming out of my shoes."*

▲ *"At first glance it may look like Magnum XL 200, but after a single scintillating circuit, you find this ride is quite unique."*

▶ *"Lofty summits, near vertical drops, and plenty of air time combine to make this the smoothest coaster ride of its kind."*

STEEL FORCE
DORNEY PARK, ALLENTOWN, PENNSYLVANIA, U.S.
Scott Rutherford

"Billed as the tallest, fastest, longest steel coaster on the East Coast of America, Steel Force is all that and a whole lot more. With 5,600 feet of track and a nearly identical paint scheme, Steel Force at first glance resembles the hyper coaster Magnum XL-200 at Cedar Point. But after a single tour of the hilly circuit, you find that the ride is quite unique. Lofty summits, near vertical drops, and plenty of air time combine with other thrilling elements to produce the smoothest steel coaster ride of its type. The 60-degree, 200-foot initial plunge into a narrow tunnel is fashioned in such a way that the elusive 'butterfly tickle' in the tummy lasts all the way to the ground. A flat mid-course brake sets the train up for a gut-wrenching drop and a perfectly paced succession of rapid camelback humps, each one producing the sensation of floating. A second tunnel leads to the startling end section, with a violent double-up maneuver, with everyone screaming and grabbing for the handhold as the train slams on the brakes.

"Congratulations to Morgan Manufacturing and Dorney Park for coming up with a world-class roller coaster that will appeal to the hard-core thrill seekers and families alike."

Ride Statistics
Steel hyper coaster, 5,600-foot track, speed 75 m.p.h., built 1997, Morgan Manufacturing.

MONTU

BUSCH GARDENS, TAMPA, FLORIDA, U.S.

Justin Garvanovic

"The descent is rapid and, before you know it, you've dropped 170 feet, turned through 200 degrees, and are heading into the first inversion. It's a superb start to the ride and leads directly into the 105-foot vertical loop. Out of the power dive, the train roars up from the ground, and into the 'immelman,' an intense reverse diving loop. Next is a fast heartline spin, then the wicked and awesome 'batwing' element which flies you out over the pit of live crocodiles. Without giving the rider time to think or blink, the train is then sent through a flat spin, and its sixth and final inversion, before heading into the high-speed spiral. This is pretty intense and is sure to leave your head buzzing.

"With tunnels and trenches to dive through as well, this is the most ingenious and spectacular ride in the world for me."

Ride Statistics

Multi-inversion suspended steel coaster, 3,983-foot track, speed 60 m.p.h., built 1996, Bolliger and Mabillard.

▲ *"Out of the power dive the train roars up from the ground and into an intense diving loop."*

▶ *"The descent is rapid and before you know it you've dropped 170 feet and heading into the first inversion."*

Tonnerre de Zeus

Parc Asterix, Plailly, Paris, France

Jean Marc Toussaint

"The morning sun breaks through the clouds as the seven-car train quietly reaches the top of the mammoth wooden structure. It suddenly dives down a 100-foot chute and I feel like I've got a five-ton monkey on my back. The silence of the lift is just a vague memory now as the monstrous racket of the wheels crunching the wood laminations becomes a deafening roar. No wonder they call it Tonnerre 'Thunder' de Zeus! In a matter of seconds we are into a heavily banked helix. The drop that follows is pure air time delight, and then we're through the tunnel, and up on the turnaround in no time. My camera is gone; its floating somewhere behind, still attached to my neck. The third drop, when it comes, is definitely the best part of the ride for me.

"As I walked through the site, on this special day, it was really weird. Less than a year ago there was nothing here but grass and trees. Now there is a monstrous wooden roller coaster, several Greek temples, flower beds, and dozens of construction people. It was a privilege to be granted one of the first rides on Tonnerre de Zeus. I can't wait to get back on it, as I live only 15 minutes away by car. No doubt I will soon be dedicating myself to the worship of Greek deities!"

Ride Statistics

Wooden out and back twister, ³/₄-mile track, speed 50 m.p.h., built 1997, Custom Coasters International.

▲ *"In a matter of seconds we were into a heavily banked helix."*

◄ *"My camera is gone, it's floating somewhere behind me, still attached to my neck."*

▲ *"We suddenly dive down a 100-foot chute and I feel like I've got a five-ton monkey on my back."*

COMET

THE GREAT ESCAPE, LAKE GEORGE, NEW YORK, U.S.

William Buckley

"One of the all-time greats was built in 1948 at Crystal Beach, Ontario, to replace the glorious Cyclone, arguably the most fearsome roller coaster ever built. In fact some of the wooden superstructure of the Cyclone was salvaged to build the Comet. What a pedigree! When Crystal Beach closed in 1989, the Comet was purchased by the owners of the Great Escape Park in Lake George. In 1994 the Philadelphia Toboggan Company rebuilt it faithfully for its new owners.

"It has a classic double out and back layout. The first drop launches the coaster like a rocket over shallow camel-hump dips on its way to the turn; the air time is phenomenal. This is repeated with bigger dips on the return leg. It's fast, breathless, and gut wrenching all the way round. The sight of the Comet structure against the trees, as you approach it, is truly inspiring.

Ride Statistics

Wooden out and back, 4,197-foot track, speed 55 m.p.h., original 1948 design by Herbert Schmeck for Crystal Beach, ride relocated in 1994.

▲ *"It has a classic out-and-back layout. It's fast, breathless, and gut-wrenching all the way round."*

▶ *"The first drop launches the coaster like a rocket over the shallow camel-hump dips."*

THRILLER
TRAVELING FAIRS IN GERMANY, E.G. OKTOBERFEST, MUNICH
Wolf Tiemeier

"I've spent most of my nonworking time, riding and writing about roller coasters in Europe, and have been on sixty-five major rides so far—a modest number compared to my coaster friends and contacts in America with whom I correspond. Like many other coaster fans, it is difficult for me to declare my all-time favorite, because I have favorites in each coaster category. For example, for wooden rides my favorite is Tonnerre de Zeus at Parc Asterix, followed by the Grand National at Blackpool. I love the scale and sheer speed of the Pepsi Max Big One and the amazing inversions and turns on Nemesis, one of the best of its kind in the world for sure.

"But I've been put on the spot so I would like to give special mention to two innovative, stunning, state-of-the-art portable steel coasters designed by Anton Schwarzkopf. They are Euro Star and Thriller. The first one is the only portable suspended coaster in the world and the second is the only portable coaster which features four different loops. Standing next to Thriller—this dream of a coaster with its gleaming red track and glistening cream supports—I forgot all the other coasters I have ever ridden. I know I was looking at the king of the coasters. It was love at first ride."

▼ *"Thriller by night, is love at first sight."*

▲ "Starting the double loop descent and the intense g
force buildup."

▲ "Flying almost vertically down the first drop of this,
the king of all coasters."

Ride Statistics

Steel, portable multi-inversion coaster, 3,300-foot track,

speed 55 m.p.h., built 1986, Schwarzkopf.

THE RAVEN

HOLIDAY WORLD, SANTA CLARA, INDIANA, U.S.

Mike Horwood

"I had heard so much about the Raven ride in the dark via the 'Stark Raven Mad' event that I had to try it for myself. You need to keep in mind that this event is scheduled when there is no moon. Other than the lights within the station, and some distant ones around the park, everything else is switched off. The ride is a coal-black, night ride, like no other that I know. By day the Raven is one of my top all-time woodies, a compelling and great ride. But the difference by night is amazing.

"You simply must plan a visit during this event, as normally this park is not open after dark, because Holiday World is a children's park. What, I ask myself, is such a wonderful ride doing in such an innocuous little park?"

Ride Statistics

Wooden out and back twister, 2,800-foot track; speed 50 m.p.h., built 1995, Custom Coasters International.

▲ *"Out of the first drop is a blind bend hidden by foliage, which catches you by surprise."*

▶ *"Looking down the first drop and the tunnel section—this compelling ride has just begun."*

◀ *"The twisted track of the Raven is very Traver-like— you're shaken, rattled, and shoved about mercilessly."*

AN INSIGHT INTO THE AMUSEMENT PARK INDUSTRY

It's quite evident when you visit an amusement park that there are different age groups taking in different attractions. It is likely that youthful, fit people will head toward white knuckle rides, while older, sedentary age groups might stroll along to the landscaped gardens or listen to a brass band. All these attractions have not happened by chance; they have all been planned. There is a strategy, a master plan, and grand design shaping, adapting, replacing, and remodeling the park to respond to the changing habits, the demographic shift, and social mores of the park-going public.

The spectacular success of the amusement park industry today mirrors the worldwide growth in tourism. In the U.S. in 1989, the amusement industry had a $4 billion turnover, with world tourism receipts topping over $2 trillion, making tourism the largest single industry in the world, with 12 percent of the world's turnover. The forecast for tourism, and for the amusement park industry, into the next century looks favorable due to the economic stability of the industrialized nations, the relatively cheap price for raw materials and energy, and the opening of international borders for trade.

New rides are being planned for the future, and many millions of dollars will be invested in a ride in the hope that it will increase the gate receipts of the park in the succeeding years. Income is needed to pay off the finance cost of a new ride, to maintain the integrity and safety of every ride, and to keep a large well-trained staff to ensure that the park runs smoothly at all times.

Every amusement park has its own unique qualities, its individual identity and character, whether it belongs to a large chain of amusement parks or is privately owned. Some amusement parks in urban locations are compressed into a small area, and packed with lots of rides. Others—better known as theme parks—are located out of the city and set in a beautiful landscape. What's so special about a park, and where it is located? What makes it different from the others? Who are the parks targeting as customers for their new multi-million dollar coaster? Is the roller coaster still the top attraction at a park?

In the second half of this chapter, we take a slice through the amusement park industry, to consider these questions, and to see how a park has evolved: how it has been forced to change and adapt, and to invest in new thrill rides and attractions.

In the first half of this chapter, we look at a typical day in the life of three amusement parks. Two are famous urban parks with a great history, and the other is a relatively new theme park, established in the 80s, and which was voted second most beautiful theme park in the world in 1996. We talk to the owners, the management, the public relations staff, and maintenance engineers, and find out what goes on behind the scenes, what's being planned, and which rides and attractions make the big impact.

KENNYWOOD—WHERE THE PAST IS THE FUTURE

Tom Maglione recalls his Kennywood memories.

Kennywood was founded in 1898 and was one of thirteen trolley parks located at the end of the line to attract passengers to ride the trolley buses in Pittsburgh during off-peak times. Kennywood is still located on its original site in the heartland of the residential neighborhood of West Mifflin, eight miles east of Pittsburgh. Over the past hundred years, the heavy industry, modes of transport, and urban infrastructure of Pittsburgh have changed beyond recognition, but not Kennywood. Kennywood's special appeal is that it has preserved the grace and style of the nineteenth century in an ever more frenetic modern world.

As a boy, I can remember eagerly anticipating my annual school picnics at a park like Kennywood, with lots of trees and picnic benches. You can still see Kennywood's picnic areas when you ride the beautiful miniature train, which has a replica Pacific locomotive pulling the carriages around the borders of the park. The train was originally built for the World Exhibition held in New York in 1939 and was brought to Kennywood shortly afterward. It now trundles past Kiddie Land, which I always find enchanting, marveling at the vintage attractions like the Auto Ride, built by Harry Traver in 1929. I revel in the childish enthusiasm and laughter of the kids driving the miniature Packard cars along a sinuous and rickety old wooden track. I still ride them myself when I visit the park. Kennywood was the first to pioneer a children's amusement park area with specifically designed rides, and it dates back to 1927. I find it reassuring to know that some things never change and that I can rekindle my own boyhood memories as I step into Kennywood.

▲ Taking the trolley bus to Kennywood Park, 1898.

▶ The wonderful Auto Ride built by Traver, 1929.

Unlike most other theme parks in North America today, Kennywood welcomes visitors who bring their own food hampers and enjoy a picnic with family and friends under the tree-covered groves within the park. I remember how the route through West Mifflin was marked with colorful yellow signs directing you all the way to the vast parking lot within Kennywood. Now this space has given way to "Lost Kennywood," built as a memorial to the great Luna Parks of Fred Ingersoll. It is complete with a replica Luna Park entrance, a shoot-the-shutes water splash named the Pittsburgh Plunge, and exotic towers and arcades all ablaze with thousands upon thousands of light bulbs. The new parking lot is situated opposite the entrance to Kennywood, which you approach via a foot tunnel under Kennywood Boulevard. The entrance brings you opposite the Turnpike built by Arrow in 1966, with its wonderful antique sports cars that run on a scaled-down roadway over bridges and through underpasses for nearly a half-mile.

But the real reason for me going to Kennywood is that within the shady picnic groves and around the artificial lake, alongside the many historical attractions, like the exquisite Denzel Carousel and the gyrating Roll-O-Plane, stand some of the most exciting and historically important roller coasters in the world. This is where I head as soon as I am through the entrance. I am a roller coaster enthusiast, a self-confessed "woodie," and this, for me, is the roller coaster capital of the world. The selection of coasters at Kennywood provides enough stimulation to satisfy any coaster fan's appetite, especially if you prefer the wooden rides like I do. Up ahead there is a sign for Kennywood's newest attraction, the "Pitt Fall." This is a 250-foot high free fall plunge that I'll just have to ride to add to my lifetime list of over 300 white knuckle rides.

The gates to the park open daily at 11 a.m., although the park staff, and the crews and ride operators, have been inside the park since dawn going through their daily routines. Two men will check the track support structures of the roller coasters, tapping in loose spikes, welding steel work, checking the chain mechanism, the train couplings, and wheels,

▲ The miniature train which takes you halfway round the park.

◀ The Thunderbolt, based on a classic design by John Miller for the Pippin.

and even oiling both rails of the Thunderbolt with an oil gun, which is quite unusual. The Thunderbolt is one of the few trains that does not have an oil sump that automatically oils the track as it coasts along. The oil helps reduce the friction between the wheels and the rails, and makes the train a faster ride. The whole park gets a clean and check-over every day, just like an office building, so that the rides are safe to run and the park is tidy and litter free.

For a gentle warm-up, my first ride of the day has to be The Racer. The stroll to The Racer will take me past the old Penny Arcade Pavilion and its collections of antique slot machines and hand-cranked movie viewers which I always enjoy. The Racer was built by John Miller in 1927 and replaced the old Racer built by Miller in 1910. Despite its second-generation tag, it is the second-oldest roller coaster operating in Kennywood today. Its two trains set off together from the station and run side by side for much of the way but end up on opposite sides of the loading station when they finish. In reality there is only one long track which makes two circuits in a clever way, allowing the two trains to race each other. There are only two other rides like this still running today but neither of them is quite as old as The Racer. This ride, with its gentle dips and sharp turns, is my mother's favorite ride. It has a large sign over the entrance to the station which is brilliantly lit up at night and which can be seen from every corner of the park.

Having got warmed up on The Racer, I then go for more exhilaration on the Jack Rabbit, which is close by and is the oldest coaster in the park. It is a classic John Miller design for an out-and-back wooden coaster, built by Miller and Baker in 1920, with 85-foot drops. It is unusual among wooden coasters because it has no lift hill at the start to pull you up and out of the station. Instead, after a brief shunt, the train turns out of the station and plunges down a ravine and then up and down a second drop before reaching the lift hill halfway round. The extra kick of going through a double drop midway through the ride is sensational. The trees hide the ravine from view and the first drop

▲ Oiling the track of Jack Rabbit and Thunderbolt, first thing every morning.

▶ The Racer lit up at night.

plunge always comes as a surprise to me, even though I have ridden the Jack Rabbit many times.

Now for the main event of the day, the Thunderbolt, which is located at the opposite end of the park and next to the Steel Phantom. By the way, the Steel Phantom holds the world record for the fastest ride and longest drop of a traditionally designed roller coaster, and is one of the best steel coaster rides in North America. All this big buildup gives me the excuse to ride the miniature train and to make a short detour to Traver's Tumble Bug, now called the Turtle, where saucer-shaped chairs, each one attached to a radius arm, are pulled along a wavy circular track that continually dips and rises. The novelty and charm of its old-world engineering is always a fascination for me. And on my way to the Thunderbolt station, I am very aware of the delightful floral displays and the well-stocked gardens *en route*, that soften the glare of the sun and the rising heat of the day. There is the floral calendar near the fountain which changes with every day, giving the date in myriad flowers. On my most recent visit, the date was picked out in white begonias set in a carpet of red salvias.

Many people have written about the Thunderbolt. In 1974 Robert Cartmell, writing as an art historian for the *New York Times*, described the thrill of riding roller coasters and its importance as the major attraction of the amusement park. He also summarized his and most other coaster connoisseurs' choice for the top coaster rides, and voted the

▲ The Pizza Pavilion with Steel Phantom in the background.

▼ The Floral Calendar at Kennywood, which changes every day.

▲ The Wave Swinger at full tilt.

▼ The Auto Ride sign at night.

Thunderbolt the greatest roller coaster ride in the world. Many coaster fans would agree with him, even today. It is certainly high on my list of all-time favorite rides. What sets the Thunderbolt apart from other woodies is the intense first drop. It is the most exhilarating first drop of any wooden coaster I have ridden. Like the Jack Rabbit, the Thunderbolt, on leaving the station, plunges down a ravine, only this drop is steeper and longer. As it tears down the ravine, it whistles under and through the first drop of the quicksilver Steel Phantom. I like to get in the front seat of the train to enjoy the uninterrupted sight of the bluffs, the Monongahela River, and the distant steel mills momentarily before being scared witless by the apparent head-on collision with the Phantom structure.

And like the Jack Rabbit, the Thunderbolt does not introduce the chain lift until halfway round. After that comes the ragdoll shake of the notorious "bowl" curves, a circular section of track that delivers intense lateral forces. The pedigree of this classic ride undoubtedly derives from John Miller's 1924 Pippin, which was rebuilt at Kennywood by Andy Vettel in 1968, following a major overhaul.

A little dizzy from all the g forces I have experienced, it is time for a snack lunch. Do I gorge on a double corn dog with salsa dip or get drawn to the frying smells of the Potato Patch and the taste of the best French fries in all America? The fries have been a major attraction at Kennywood for many years, with customers coming here rather than another park just to eat them! On an average day, patrons will munch through one ton of potatoes but at peak times the Potato Patch staff peel, wash, hand press, and deep fry two and a half tons of these enormous golden-brown fingers. I like to eat mine sitting by the lakeside which provides a good vantage point of Kennywood.

From this point, you can locate many of Kennywood's landmarks, while working out the afternoon or evening ride agenda. The vista grows especially appealing when the sun sets. I don't like the spinning rides any more so, for someone like me, sitting by the lakeside awhile is a wise move. Then I might go souvenir hunting and visit the Penny Arcade to roll a penny, flip a bagatelle pin, or lose my small change in the cranky old slot machines, all the while reveling in the nostalgia of these cherished pastimes. I may even take a turn on the old Grand Prix bumper cars to warm up again for yet more coaster rides.

In my youth I would have cooled down in the midday sun by diving and swimming around in Kennywood's vast 160- by 120-yard pool, then stretching out on the artificial beach built alongside it. The giant pool closed in the late 1950s. Today, if you want to get wet, you ride the Raging Rapids or Log Jammer or, if you don't mind getting soaked, take the Pittsburgh Plunge, a water ride that creates huge splashes. Although wet rides, like the Log Jammer, claim to be the equivalent of a roller coaster ride, they seem rather tame to me. But 24,000 people might just have a point—that's the number of people who enjoy the water rides on a peak day.

My favorite noncoaster ride at Kennywood is Le Cachot (that's French for "the dungeon"), a haunted house ride that's only a little scary. The motorized carts can seat two large

▼ The Pitt Fall, Kennywood's latest white knuckle, is a free fall plunge from 200 feet.

or three slim riders, and travel through a maze of darkened rooms with various mechanized contraptions that flash, pop out, or dangle over you unexpectedly. It is a classic dark ride and I know very few modern parks that offer this kind of spooky ride, although there are modern attractions like it at Disneyland and Alton Towers.

As an adult I still enjoy a ride in the gentle "tunnel of love," which was once named Harold's Horrendous Humorous Haunted Hideaway. It is now called the Old Mill. I also like to visit old Noah's Ark. It arrived in Kennywood in 1936, the same year that Pittsburgh was devastated by the worst floods the city has ever experienced. It is one of the three surviving Noah's Arks in the world today. The other two are located at Blackpool Pleasure Beach, Blackpool, and Frontierland Western Theme Park in Morecambe, England. The original entrance was through a whale's mouth which led onto a log-stump pathway. As you stepped on the logs, a jet of air was released which blew up the ladies' skirts. Inside was a small "haunted" house with animals and snakes that jumped out at you. The original structure was completely renovated in 1996, and there is now a new entrance called the Elevator of Doom and a lot of new hi-tech thrills inside the Ark.

As the day turns to night, the sky comes alive with twinkling and sparkling lights from all over the park. The incandescence of the many hues, some neon and some filament bulbs, pick out the silhouettes of the trees and the attractions. They follow the rotation of the rides, spilling their myriad colors onto the watery reflections of the lake. At about

► Fun, frolics, and hi-tech thrills on the revamped Noah's Ark, one of only three left in the world.

▲ The glorious Denzel Carousel.

this time, lots of people gather on the lakeside to enjoy a variety show, set on the grand stage in the middle of the lake. The show features many stunt acts—my favorite is a man being shot out of a cannon across the lake and into a safety net on the other side. There is always a parade or festival of some sort in July and August that finishes with a fireworks display. I particularly like the Fall Fantasy Parade in late August, where wonderfully illuminated floats, school bands, and costumed entertainers parade around the lake.

Inevitably the fun has to come to an end and, in a long-standing Kennywood tradition, it is always a "soft closing time." That means that Kennywood will stay open for longer than the scheduled time on those balmy summer evenings, as long as everyone is still having fun. The final closing is heralded by the playing of the Kennywood anthem, which wishes everyone goodnight and goodbye. Memories of a good time endure and I know I shall return to rekindle youthful dreams once again, and to ride the Thunderbolt and the Steel Phantom.

A Day in the Life of Blackpool Pleasure Beach

You may go to an amusement park for a variety of reasons, but underpinning your motives is the sense of fun, of pleasure, and excitement of being at a fairground with a host of attractions that will never bore! Your social background and status may draw you to a particular park, where the accent may be on scenic spaces, themed feature areas, and

water gardens, as well as white knuckle rides. Some may prefer the tightly packed centers like Blackpool Pleasure Beach, a 42-acre park paved in concrete and tarmac, screened by various steel and wooden constructions, infused with a cocktail of cooking smells, constant noise, and the buzz of the attractions enticing you at every step.

What hits the senses as you walk through the turnstiles at Blackpool is the distant outline of the biggest and tallest ride in the park, an irresistible calling bird to which your eyes are drawn like a magnet ... a roller coaster, the Pepsi Max Big One. It's the big ride that sets the pulses racing and the adrenaline flowing, and people all react quite differently as they approach. Some pull away from their friends, too frightened to go on, only to be coaxed and bullied to stay with assurances that it's a tame ride. Some people rub their hands in anticipation as they wait their turn in the line-up, some talk animatedly, some appear calm but are suffering great internal stress and trying not to show it.

We could see the monster curve of the first and second drop four miles away. Only Blackpool Tower was more imposing on the skyline, and I was thrilled. We were a middle-aged, middle-class group of people, traveling in the cushioned luxury of a decent automobile, about to confront our worst fears. None of us had been to Blackpool in the past twenty years nor ever wanted to since our childhood days. It was, after all, a holiday resort for the working classes, full of garish arcades, boarding house signs, bingo calling houses,

▲ The outline of the Pepsi Max Big One, viewed from John Miller's Big Dipper.

◀ *"Hold onto your seats!"* Looking down the first drop of the Pepsi Max Big One at Blackpool Pleasure Beach.

▶ Blackpool Pleasure Beach, England, c.1930. In the background is the L.A. Thompson Scenic Railway (1907).

tacky snack bars with plastic garlic plants, tasteless postcards, sickly toffee apples, and donkey droppings on a dun-colored beach that stretched for miles along a promenade trundling with vintage trams, ponies and traps, and more horse smells. And the Pleasure Beach is stuck right in the middle of it.

Only two of my less cowardly friends had the courage to ride any of the white knuckle rides with me but even they refused to go anywhere near the Pepsi Max Big One, despite all the buildup and pep-talking I gave them before we arrived. This is the "Mecca," I explained, for the classic coaster rides, the place of the legends in the coaster world where Henry Iles built L A Thompson's Scenic Railway, where John Miller's glorious Velvet Coaster and Big Dipper were built by Bill Strickler, where Harry Traver helped Charlie Paige construct the famous Grand National, where Arrow built their first corkscrew coaster—the Revolution—outside the U.S., and designed the novel Steeplechase ride, and the awesome steel hyper coaster—the Pepsi Max Big One.

Blackpool today stands for much more than roller coaster history. The compact 42-acre site is a working museum of amusement park history, with a myriad of mechanical rides, fun palaces, water attractions, restaurants, casinos, and arcades, whose origins can be traced back over a hundred years to the days of William Bean, who established a funfair on the dunes of Blackpool beach in 1896. He would be proud to have seen what the family business has achieved since then. His daughter, Mrs. Doris Thompson, who was born in 1903, and is the mother of the current chairman Geoffrey Thompson, still comes to the park in her chauffeur-driven Rolls-Royce most days.

"We wanted to found an American-style amusement park, the fundamental principle of which is to make adults feel like children again, and to inspire gaiety of a primarily innocent nature," explained Doris Thompson. "But let's not forget that Blackpool is a working-class holiday resort for the people of Lancashire, Cheshire, Yorkshire, and the

▲ William Bean, the founder of Blackpool Pleasure Beach.

▶ An aerial view of the Pleasure Beach, 1935.

north of England, and Blackpool Pleasure Beach is one of the principal attractions of their summer vacation. That is our core market, but of course we attract visitors from all over the country, mainland Europe and the U.S. They come to the Pleasure Beach because we have the biggest collection of historic roller coaster rides, the entry is free, we have lots of shows and evening entertainment, and we have the Pepsi Max Big One."

Doris Thompson last rode a roller coaster in 1994, but she was game enough to free fall 200 feet on the new £2 million Play Station that opened in June 1997, to raise money for her favorite charity. Some lady.

If I had to choose the best ride at Blackpool, then it would have to be the Grand National. It was built in 1935 and was modeled on the lines of the famous Cyclone Racer that Harry Traver had built for Fred Church, over Pike Pier at Long Beach, California, in 1930. The Cyclone Racer was arguably one of the most beautiful and evocative timber structures ever built for a roller coaster.

How good is the ride? A quote from an article written by Mary Jackson that appeared in *First Drop* magazine about her childhood memories of Blackpool reveals all. "I'm not sure who was more nervous, me, my Dad, or my Mum as we queued for the ride. Once we got on the ride all I can remember thinking is 'I want to get off.' As we got to the top

▲ The Play Station, the Pleasure Beach's latest attraction, is a freefall plunge of 200 feet.

of the lift, it was twilight and the illuminations were on along the beach front. From up there I had the best view of the lights and the sea that I had ever seen. Then, I remembered where I was and suddenly we were hurtling down the first drop and the whole thing seemed to be over in one long scream. It was the most terrifying thing that I had ever experienced in my life. When I got off the ride I could hardly walk, nor could my Dad for that matter. My Mum who had shut her eyes all the way round finally opened them. Never again I said to myself, but that was short lived. I have been a woodie addict ever since and the Grand National is my favorite ride."

According to Keith Allan, the operations manager, the £12 million Pepsi Max Big One is the top ride earner, carrying 1,800 persons per hour and netting £7,200 an hour at peak times. "We had to rebuild the first drop of the Big One last year at a cost of £800,000, because the twist at the top of the first drop was too sharp. It would be nice to think that once we've built a new ride we don't have to spend any more on it! Far from it. We employ a huge staff, to maintain and to operate the rides. Every morning before the Pleasure Beach opens, fifty electricians and mechanics are out on the rides checking every inch of the track, the structure, and the cars for loose bolts, worn track, wheel bearing wear, or any structural damage which could impair the safety and efficiency of the ride, and which must be put right before the park opens."

It is the park's worst nightmare to have to close down a ride following an accident or incident which has put the safety of passengers at risk. Think of the revenue that could be lost. Thursday, July 7, 1994, at 4 p.m. in the afternoon was a black day for the Pleasure Beach, when two trains on the Pepsi Max Big One crashed into each other, injuring twenty-six people. Firemen had to cut free the people who were trapped in the wreckage of the cars. Fortunately no one was seriously injured, but the Health and Safety Executive shut the ride down until they were satisfied that the computer fault and brake failure which caused it could never happen again.

Geoffrey Thompson, the chairman of the Pleasure Beach, was at a loss to explain why the cars had crashed. "The manufacturers were incredulous when we told them. They said that there was no way it could happen. We have an excellent safety record for all our rides. It is very, very high indeed. If other means of public transport had our record of safety, I think they would be very proud people."

As we walked around the park, we were aware of the number of "ride-on" mini road sweepers that were snaking their way through the crowds. Every day there are twelve park rangers cleaning some part of the many miles of walkways of rubbish, spilled drinks, butt ends, dropped food, and the like, or emptying the many trash cans. On an average day they will empty 1,500 trash cans and clear away twelve tons of debris.

▲ Emberton's station for the Grand National is a glorious piece of modern architecture.

◄ The Grand National layout is a gem; the ride is quick, tummy-tingling, and one long screaming laugh all the way round.

▲ The Big Dipper tower and entrance lit up at night.

"And that is not all as we clear up," Keith Allen reflected with a sense of fun. "Two years ago we drained the pool below the Pepsi Max Big One and Big Dipper to carry out some maintenance on the Log Flume. We found all sorts of personal effects on the bottom. They had dropped or fallen while taking one of the rides. We counted 180 sets of false teeth, numerous combs, wallets, spectacles, sunglasses, and a glass eye which was later reclaimed by the owner who had reported it missing to one of the park rangers, leaving his name and address."

After an excellent lunch of fish, chips, and mushy peas at the Fish Inn—one of many restaurants that front the curving white Wonderful World Building—I rode John Miller's Big Dipper. Having done the Pepsi Max Big One before lunch, and been numbed by the 4 g pumping through my arms as they gripped the safety bar, it was a delight to be able to feel, to absorb, and to reconcile "brain with body" as I plunged the drops and hugged the turns of the Big Dipper. To me the Pepsi Max Big One was a cold, colorless ride where all the negative g had been harnessed out of it because of the way you are strapped in. It was also too fast and unforgiving to be enjoyed the first time round. I'm told by coaster buffs that you have to ride the Big One four or five times before you enjoy it! Well for the £20 that you might have to fork out to punish yourself, why bother when you could have a far better time riding the Grand, the Big Dipper, the Wild Mouse, and the novel Steeplechase ride more than once?

▼ The really wild Wild Mouse, a wooden track coaster, built 1958.

◀ The Steeplechase, built to commemorate the Grand National, England's most famous horse race.

▼ The Wonderful World building, repainted white in 1996 to mark Blackpool Pleasure Beach's centenary.

The day was gray and cool, with the threat of rain in the wind. By mid-afternoon we thought our luck was running out and decided to finish the day with first a ride on the Steeplechase—a ride where the women joined the men for the first time—and then the Log Flume. For collective fun, novelty, moments of exhilaration, tummy tingling laughter, and romance, you can't beat the Steeplechase, another of the hidden treasures in the Pleasure Beach. It was designed by Frank Wright of Arrow Developments in 1977 and consists of single horses fitted with wheels that run on a steel track, each horse capable of carrying two riders, and racing each other on three parallel tracks around a figure-eight that is a half-mile long. The idea was dreamed up by the current park owner Geoffrey Thompson who was inspired by the fact that Liverpool was the home of Britain's greatest horse race, the Grand National, and that Blackpool was the training ground of Red Rum, the greatest horse to run the National. The Steeplechase was a wonderful idea and opened in the same year that Red Rum won the National for a third time!

When we got off our last ride, the Log Flume, we were soaked to the skin, shoes squeaking with water, and hair matted over our heads. And as we stood looking like drowned rats, we did not have a care in the world. We all said in one breath "What fun, why don't we all ride the Grand National!" Suddenly we were free of our worries, our back problems, muscle strain, the height of the Big One, and the superficiality of the park. We loved the Pleasure Beach, the garish signs, the laughing clown, the sirens and jangling noises, and the smells, and understood its special appeal and why it draws 7.5 million visitors a year to it.

▲ Nemesis, the ultimate experience, an adrenaline-filled, 50 m.p.h. cartwheel.

▲ "You won't catch me on this ride." The Ripsaw at Alton Towers.

▲ "Wear swim wear, keep your eyes shut, and take a seasickness pill if you want to enjoy the Ripsaw!"—that's my advice!

A DAY IN THE LIFE OF ALTON TOWERS, ALTON, STAFFORDSHIRE, ENGLAND

For those who have not been to a theme park with a reputation for beautiful landscaped gardens, tasteful setting, and sensitive layouts, as well as its roller coaster rides, please make every effort to visit one if you can. These are the Gardens of Eden of the amusement park world, the quintessential example of which is Alton Towers in Staffordshire, in the heart of England.

There is no other theme park that can boast a thousand years of history, or of an estate of five hundred acres where the great Earl Talbot, who had fought alongside Henry V at Agincourt, had made his home. Here the renowned architects Augustus Welby Pugin and James Wyatt were hired to work their architectural magic in creating the Gothic splendor of Alton Towers between the seventeenth and eighteenth centuries for the wealthy 15th and 16th Earls of Shrewsbury. They transformed a large country residence into a grand palace mansion without parallel in the architectural history of England.

Until his death in 1827, the 15th Earl, Charles Talbot, devoted much of his time and a considerable part of his enormous financial resources creating the magnificent gardens that we can enjoy today. By the mid-eighteenth century, Alton Towers was one of the most splendid houses and landscaped gardens in all of England. The landscaped gardens of Alton Towers compare with the famous gardens of Stowe and Stourhead, and were replete with a miniature "Stonehenge," many ornate and unusual fountains, an orangery, and a conservatory with seven glass domes. The vast sweeps of the Rock Gardens at the head of the valley are packed with rhododendrons, azaleas, and other magnificent flowering shrubs and trees that cover this landscape in a thousand colors.

But the buildings of Alton Towers today are just empty shells, devoid of their ornate interiors and splendid furnishings, having fallen into disrepair after their contents were auctioned off to pay for the enormous legal cost in contesting the ownership of the estate when the 17th Earl died childless in 1857.

After the Second World War, the estate was sold to Alton Towers Ltd., and in 1980 John Broome inherited the controlling shares and turned it into the first theme park in England. It was the energy and enterprise of John Broome that was responsible for introducing the American concept of a theme park with thrill rides, and a one-price ticket entry, to Britain. Since the Tussaud's Group acquired the park in 1991, they have added the awesome steel suspended coaster Nemesis, the exhilarating Runaway Mine Train, the twisting, rotating Ripsaw and Energizer, and the wonderful worlds of Storybook Land and Old MacDonald's Farm. They have been refurbishing rides like the Beast, Black Hole, Corkscrew, and Log Flume, and the other attractions they inherited from John Broome's company and have made great improvements to the amenities within the park.

When you experience Alton Towers for the first time it is the little things that make it such a special day. For instance the welcoming voice of Malcolm the Monorail, who tells you that he never breaks down as you journey to the main park entrance from the parking lot complex. Then there are the crowd-free walkways that link you to the themed areas, the siting of the rides below the tree line or in hollows surrounded by trees entirely hidden from view, the colorful sculptured forms that surround some of the rides like the dragon monster sprawling over Nemesis and standing in pools of red-dyed water.

No matter how well we tried to plan our day, we never managed to get to all the attractions, let alone visit the historic Tower. How could we pass up the opportunity to ride the fabulous Runaway Mine Train at least six times, as there was no waiting or the wicked Log Flume ride twice in succession, without getting off? Then we stood for some time laughing at the riders mad enough to be spun and rotated in the giant wheel of the Ripsaw before being completely drenched while hanging upside-down. It is the most fearsome white knuckle ride I have ever seen.

But if I had to name my favorite experience at Alton Towers, it has to be Storybook Land and Old MacDonald's Farm, where you are greeted by the sleepy but erudite Bookworm at the press of a button. He told us all about the delights of Storybook Land while looking at us over his spectacles with his large saucer eyes. And who can forget the animated, life-size animals in the interactive signing barn—the cow, the hens on eggs, old MacDonald and his shaking tractor, the horse, the grunting pig, the barking dog, the hooting owl, and the bleating billy goat—all singing *Old MacDonald Had A Farm* if you pressed the

▲ The gothic spires of Alton Towers and the lake.

▼ Old McDonald's singing barn in Storybook Land.

▲ *"With an oink, oink here and an oink, oink there"* sings Mr. Pig, at the push of a button.

▲ The landscaped gardens of Six Flags Over Georgia.

▼ The graceful sweeps of the Great American Scream Machine.

▶ Mind Bender, a terrific steel coaster, tearing down the first drop into oblivion.

red timer knob that sprung them into action. We were joined by four other adults to keep all the animals singing simultaneously, and we had such a laugh.

We were the oldest kids in the park that day and want to come back in spring to see the blossom. To hide our embarrassment next time we visit Storybook Land, we will be bringing our young niece along. Alton Towers is a magical place and has something there for everyone to enjoy. It is Britain's most popular theme park, with 2.5 million visitors a year, and I can understand why.

SIX FLAGS THEME PARKS INC. AND THE COASTER THEME PARK

The first big theme park, along with Knott's Berry Farm, to compete successfully with Disneyland was Six Flags Over Texas at Arlington, between Dallas and Forth Worth. It was the brainchild of Angus Wynne, and opened in 1961, covering thirty-five acres. The park was segmented into six theme areas, each one representing the flag countries or states that once occupied Texas: Spain, France, Mexico, the Republic Of Texas, the Confederacy, and the United States. But quite deliberately, and in contrast with Disney, the thrill rides were given center stage and were liberally planned in each sector. A log flume splashes through the Spanish rapids, a runaway mine train races through the Confederacy, a wooden roller coaster hurtles through the United States. Entertainment and high activity mixed with plush landscaped areas were the feature of all the other Six Flag Parks from the beginning, and a single, all-in-one admission price gave unlimited access to the rides and attractions.

Six Flags Over Georgia, the third in the Six Flags chain, which opened in 1967, embodied the emerging modern theme park concept. It was located along an interstate highway, encouraging the patronage of families because a car was needed to get to the park. The routing of the main road and highways system plays an important role, since the parks are bonded to the automobile as the primary means of access. The baby boomers of the 1950s, now in middle age, are the principal target of the regional theme parks, as are the parents with children in tow. They would not be lured to an urban attraction where crime, unsupervised youths, and rowdy elements would have easy access. Cleanliness and hospitality were also paramount, as well as extensive picnic areas and attractive gardens to extol the family values of the park. There was an enchanted woodland, a kiddie zoo, and the Crystal Music Hall, all set in a 300-acre garden.

But unlike the traditional city-based or seafront amusement park, which enticed urban and city dwellers with fabulous lights and lots of noise, such as Blackpool Pleasure Beach, Astroland, and Kennywood, the regional theme parks were very understated on arrival, often hidden from view behind a buffer zone of trees, shrubs, and high walls. The buffer zone or high fence reinforces the sense of protection, and the promise of paradise within that is so essential to the success of the park.

That is why Six Flags Over Georgia is located some distance from Atlanta. "We started off with the rolling hills of Georgia and a natural terrain that was so unbelievably beautiful" says Spurgeon Richardson, general manager of Six Flags Over Georgia, talking to *At The Park* editor Allen Ambrosini, "We tried to work around that, to make that a big plus for us."

It is one of the most striking aspects of the park, which ranks alongside Busch Gardens, Williamsburg, as one of the most beautiful theme parks in the U.S. Landscaping staff work long hours to keep the shrubs, the perennial, and annual flowers at their peak throughout the year, often changing plants three to four times in a season. It's no small wonder that so many visitors come to Six Flags Over Georgia just to see the flowers.

And as the roller coaster bonanza took hold of the U.S. in the 70s, so Six Flags Over Georgia, like the other Six Flags parks, invested in monster rides of high speed and big thrills. The Great American Scream Machine, with a first drop of 85 feet, rose out from a tranquil lake to claim the title of longest wooden coaster in the world in 1973. Intamin and Schwarzkopf were contracted to design and build the breathtaking Mind Bender shortly afterward, a magnificent triple looping coaster voted by many coaster buffs as one of their favorite steel rides. And then in 1990 the Georgia Cyclone was introduced to the park. It was a copy of the famous Coney Island Cyclone, but with a replica of the Cyclone at Astroland, Coney Island, and the Texas Cyclone at Astroworld already up and running, why build yet another version of the same ride?

"What we tried to do was to take the thrills of the original Coney Island Cyclone and combine it with today's technology of improved cars and track construction" responds Richardson. "We built the Georgia Cyclone ten feet taller as well. It has proved to be a sound investment and is easily the most exciting roller coaster in south east America today. We feel it is one of the top five roller coaster rides in the country. There are ten spots of air time on the ride and I love the intensity of it."

Six Flags Over Georgia are in a tough competitive market and arguably the most competitive location for a theme park anywhere in the world, with Busch Gardens, Disney, EPCOT, Universal Studios, Sea World, Dollywood, Opryland, and Carowinds nearby. "The bottom line is you've got to give people reasons to come back to the park every year" says Richardson. "That reason might be different from year to year. For example this year, the Cyclone, with its appeal to the twelve and twenty-four age group, extended the demographic reach to a wider age group because a lot of older people have heard about the original Cyclone or had ridden that ride and wanted to come out here to experience it for themselves."

Six Flags stretched the original Disneyland theme park concept. The overwhelming financial success of Six Flags Parks year after year set the stage for a burgeoning industry once again and spawned the regional theme park revolution. In the spring of 1998 Six Flags Theme Parks Inc. was acquired by Premier Parks Inc.

▶ The Georgia Cyclone, a faithful copy of the famous Coney Island Cyclone, only bigger.

CEDAR POINT, SANDUSKY, OHIO, U.S.

Cedar Point is one of the best known amusement parks of North America; it boasts one of the greatest stretches of beach and the luxurious Breakers Hotel, as well as being home to a fabulous collection of high-speed, spine-tingling steel and wooden roller coasters. Many coaster fans would argue that Cedar Point has two of the best rides of their kind in the U.S., in the 80-m.p.h. steel rapier Magnum XL-200, built in 1989, and the sleek, green, suspended invertor Raptor, built in 1994.

Cedar Point did not happen overnight, no big money nor frantic building program could ever have transformed such a barren, dune covered, rocky peninsular on the edge of Lake Erie in 1870, into the mature, sophisticated pleasure land of 364 acres it is today. The development and continual search for novelty attractions, for thrilling rides, family entertainment, and fun takes many years to evolve. What you see at Cedar Point today is the culmination of many years of planning, of brilliant design ideas, and serious money gambled on the building of rides that will sustain the park's success and satisfy the public demand for spectacular thrills and spills.

◀ Blue Streak, a John Allen designed, out-and-back wooden coaster.

▲ Cedar Point on the horizon, approached on the Sandusky Bridge, in the early 1900s.

Cedar Point, the old man of the amusement park world, with the longest survival record, reinvented itself in the 60s and 70s in order to keep pace with the fashion for theme parks that had emerged with Disney and the Six Flags Corporation. Under the direction of Robert Mungers in the 70s and Richard Kinzel later in the 80s, Cedar Point began to focus much of its expansion and capital improvements program installing a collection of state-of-the-art roller coasters, like no other park in the world. From once being named the "Queen of America's Watering Places," Cedar Point metamorphosed into the "Amazement Park" and was dubbed the Rollercoaster Capital of the World, with twelve stupendous roller coasters—eight steel and two wooden—a bobsled, and two mine trains, besides a host of other entertainment features, park lands, and a beach resort.

The Corkscrew was the first of the revolutionary scream machines to appear in the park sometime after John Allen's handsome out and back woodie Blue Streak was finished in 1964. It was a looping steel coaster which was the first Arrow design to incorporate a 360-degree corkscrew. It opened in 1976 amid much publicity and media attention. The brilliant-white steel arches and twisting red track of the Corkscrew creates a dramatic entry to Cedar Point, permitting patrons to walk directly under the corkscrew element whose toboggans spiral through at nearly 50 m.p.h.

Next came the gigantic Gemini coaster in 1978, a twin track, upright, steel racing coaster built to mimic the appearance of a wooden coaster ride. It was the tallest coaster in the world when it opened, standing at 128 feet. On a clear night, so they say, the lights on Gemini can be seen for many miles out across Lake Erie. Gemini was the first

▼ Robert Mungers.

▶ The eye-catching structure of the Arrow suspended coaster Iron Dragon, at Cedar Point.

▶ The magnificent Magnum XL 200, a hyper coaster designed by Arrow, described as "mind altering, stupefying, and other dimensional."

◀ *Magnum facts:* hyper steel coaster; 5,106-foot track; lift hill 205 foot; max speed 72 m.p.h.; ride capacity 2,000 rides/hour; cost $8 million; built in 1989.

◀ *Raptor facts:* multi-inversion outside looping suspended steel coaster; 3,790-foot track; lift hill 137 feet; max speed 57 m.p.h.; ride capacity 1,800 rides/hour; cost $11.5 million; built in 1994.

◀ *Mean Streak facts:* out-and-back classic wooden coaster; 5,427-foot; lift hill 161 feet; max speed 65 m.p.h.; ride capacity 1,600 rides/hour, cost $7.5 million; built in 1991.

◀ *Ripcord facts:* it is not a roller coaster but a free fall jump from tower over 300 feet high, with single riders harnessed to a cable that "flies" the rider as it plummets down to the landing point.

of only two large-scale, wood structured, tubular-tracked coasters to be built in the world, and has become a firm favorite of coaster fans. The 3,935-foot long track starts with a stomach-grabbing first drop of 118 feet, ducks under the coaster structure, and generates a speed approaching 60 m.p.h. The ride finishes in a snappy spiral and gives a ride duration of two minutes and twenty seconds.

Iron Dragon was next in the stable, a steel suspended coaster designed for fun rather than thrills, with an esthetic beauty all its own. The coaster starts the first half of the ride by weaving its way through a wooded island, then emerges out over a mist-shrouded lagoon, performing aerobatics, before running into its uniquely themed station building. Built in 1987, it has a track length of 2,800 feet and a first drop of 76 feet.

Ranked by readers of roller coaster magazines as North America's best steel roller coaster, the Magnum XL-200, designed by Arrow in 1989, is also one of the fastest in the world. So successful has it been for its owners at Cedar Point that the Thompson family had it copied for Blackpool Pleasure Beach and named it the Pepsi Max Big One. Roller coaster enthusiast and magazine editor Allen Ambrosini said this about the Magnum: "Want some descriptive words about Magnum? How about: mind altering, stupefying, hair raising, ferocious, humungus, ultimate, other dimensional, Olympian! OK?"

Two years later came Mean Streak, the last roller coaster designed by the legendary team of Curtis Summers and Charlie Dinn in 1991, a year before Summers died. Mean Streak has the menace of the classic wooden coaster of the 30s, with sheer walls of timber, some 160 feet high, creating gigantic tableaux of curving timber tapestries that follow the snaking trail of the thrilling track layout. The layout makes the track criss-cross nine times on itself, and twist and dip twelve times, as it speeds its screaming passengers at 65 m.p.h. up and over two hills 100 feet high, before slamming on the brakes to its journey's end. Mean Streak goes fast, and this is no small ride. It is the world's tallest wooden coaster and has the second longest wooden track length in the world of 5,427 feet, which is over a mile.

And just when you thought Cedar Point had run out of ideas and money, and needed time to consolidate their amazing collection of rides, along comes Raptor. It is a gorgeous, green, sleek marvel of engineering, a spectacular suspended steel coaster with six inversions, vertical loops, and a cobra roll which turns riders upside-down twice. The outside looping coaster gives the feel of flight, generating high negative g over a stunning tubular steel support layout, that was designed and built by Bolliger and Mabillard in 1994. Riders are suspended ski-lift style, with shoulder harness and lap belt, and arranged four abreast as they fly the 3,790-foot layout, which has a longest drop of 119 feet, and a maximum speed of 57 m.p.h. For some coaster fans, this is the most thrilling ride experience at Cedar Point.

Then in 1996 Mantis was unveiled, a stand-up coaster by Bolliger and Mabillard, which was the twelfth coaster project at Cedar Point and the first stand-up coaster with a dive

▲ The Corkscrew, the first Arrow looping coaster to deploy a 360-degree corkscrew roll.

▶ The lumbering structure of Gemini stretches out to the shoreline of Lake Eerie. Its wooden structure disguises its tubular steel running tracks.

▶ Raptor, a marvel of steel engineering and numbing g forces, designed by Bolliger & Mabillard for Cedar Point, 1994.

loop, and inclined loop. The fastest ride of its kind, it reaches 60 m.p.h. at the base of the first drop.

Thirty-seven million dollars was sanctioned by Mungers from 1968 through 1979 to help Cedar Point into the top ten most visited parks in the U.S., ahead of Six Flags Over Georgia, Busch Gardens, Williamsburg, and Six Flags Magic Mountain. Along with plans to concentrate on building major rides every two years, Cedar Point management has maintained an exceptional capital expenditure program to reinvest substantial profits back into the park. Care to preserve the past is also evident in the restored street furniture, the lamp posts, park benches, and castiron sculptures, and artefacts. Cedar Point is a blend of the old and new, of thrilling white knuckle rides mixed with the nostalgia of carefree summer days, open spaces, a spectacular lake shore, and good clean fun without the artificiality of city-based parks.

BUFFALO BILL'S RESORT CASINO AND THE DESPERADO

If you are enthralled, intoxicated, and wedded to the whole ethos of the roller coaster experience then Buffalo Bill's Resort Casino would be the place to spend your dying days. In the flat, dry Nevada Valley miles from anywhere with just the vultures, a parched mountain range, prairie dogs, and cacti for company, stands a fifteen-story gingerbread building encircled by a badly made spider's web painted bright yellow—it's the Desperado, the tallest, fastest hyper coaster in the world.

▲ Buffalo Bill's Resort and the Desperado.

As the day temperature outside gets too hot for comfort—it is a desert after all—the management decided that it would be fun to give their customers a few interesting indoor diversions, as a respite from the 1,669 slot machines, forty-six gambling tables, the buffalo-shaped swimming pool, water slides, and gourmet restaurants. One of these diversions almost leaps out of the fourth floor of the chocolate colored façade and panda white window frames of the Buffalo Bill's hotel.

Gary Primm, the owner of the Buffalo Bill's and a cluster of other buildings that form part of his 800-acre estate in the desert, approached Ron Toomer of Arrow in 1993 with an interesting proposition.

> "Build me the world's tallest and fastest roller coaster that will travel round and through a new twin block hotel of 1,220 luxury bedrooms, which I am going to call Buffalo Bill's Resort Casino. Oh, by the way, I have $10 million for the project!"

Ron Toomer and his Arrow team could hardly believe their luck. There is no other roller coaster quite like the Desperado. Its sheer scale and audacious conception defy description. And not even pictures give you the full impact of this towering, skipping rope structure, against the bright blue Nevada sky. It is a piece of post-romantic architecture with a longest drop of 225 feet, track length of 5,840 feet, and a top speed of 80 m.p.h.

Because of the extreme temperatures outdoors, it was practical to house the coaster station in the hotel, straddling the twin blocks and the glass atrium that covers the first floor concourse and magnificent pool. It had to be an air-conditioned station, of course, so that you could wake up in the morning, get the elevator to the fourth floor, step into the bright-yellow cars of the Desperado, and view the vast Nevada landscape and the Buffalo Bill Resort at 70-m.p.h., with the rising sun. What a start to the day, what a wake-up call, and with the pulse rate quickly up to 150 it surely must be classed as two and half minutes of exhilarating exercise. Follow this with a quick shower, breakfast, some black jack, slot machines, another 70-m.p.h. ride, a swim before lunch at the Baja Grill perhaps, a snooze, a few beers, another 70-m.p.h. ride ... What a way to spend the day!

The Desperado is the only roller coaster at Buffalo Bill's resort and was created to add to the attractions for the young at heart, and to encourage families to stop over to enjoy the resort facilities. The main business is the casino complex, but the impact and stunning structure of the Desperado has become such a successful advertising symbol that it has promoted the ride and the resort all over the U.S. and the world.

Here a roller coaster has been used as a decoy to catch the interest and curiosity of some 10.5 million cars that travel on Interstate I-15, between Los Angeles and Las Vegas. Studies have shown that 20 percent of all cars stop at least once at the resort, staying overnight at Buffalo Bill's, Whiskey Pete's, or the Primadonna. That gives the resort a powerful advantage as it has a virtual monopoly at its border location, strategically situated between LA and Vegas.

Stateline, Nevada was once a dustbowl with a two-pump gas station and a twelve-room truck driver motel. Gary Primm, the entrepreneur, and his co-investors, have turned this dustbowl into a fabulous gaming resort that now boasts 2,700 rooms, 3,500 employees, a 6,500-seater arena where Bob Dylan, B. B. King, and the Moody Blues have played concerts, a movie theater, three video arcades, an eighteen-hole golf course, a log flume ride, a 200-foot turbo drop, and the Desperado.

ELITCH GARDENS

It is strange to witness a famous urban park get the removal vans in and relocate the rides, the fun houses, and everything else no more than fifty miles down the road, after a hundred years of success on the original site. Why not keep the old one open and run both parks? According to the owners of Elitch Gardens, the move from just outside Denver to inside the city limits will ensure the survival of Elitch Gardens in the future. But why become an urban park served by a public transport system which can attract the criminal element, rowdy youths and turn family customers away?

At one time Elitch Gardens was a competitor to the great Coney Island parks in the 20s, ranking in popularity with Euclid Beach (Cleveland), Kennywood (Pittsburgh), and Pike Pier (Los Angeles). It was only one of seven established parks to survive the crash of the 30s, the impact of the Disney empire, and the theme park era that followed in the 70s. Several famous names had already been swept into oblivion during this period—

▲ The yellow peril, the Desperado, the fastest gravity roller coaster in the world, its ribbon support structure silhouetted against the Nevada skyline.

Luna, Steeplechase, Revere Beach, Crystal Beach, Riverside, Palisades, and Dreamland Park, to name but a few. They either burnt down, closed from lack of patronage, fell into neglect and had to be shut, or succumbed to the condo developers' advance.

Elitch Gardens started off as a sixteen-acre fruit and vegetable farm run by John and Mary Elitch, that grew into a zoo and picnic gardens, opening to the public in 1890. The compact site developed into an historic Colorado landmark of twenty-eight acres for more than a century, entertaining visitors in its elaborate gardens, old-style theater, the Trocadero ballroom, symphony orchestra concerts, and, not least, the thrill rides. Over the years its popularity grew, until in the 1990s a million people had packed into this small park. Each year brought more saturation, overcrowding and inevitable tales of discontent amongst patrons. Elitch Gardens had outgrown its site and needed a land area twice the size fast, if it was going to survive.

October 1, 1994, was the last day of the old Elitch Gardens. Twelve thousand people came to the park that day to say farewell to 104 years of history, and to ride John Allen's greatest woodie, Mr. Twister, and Herb Schmeck's wonderful Wildcat for the last time, before they were dismantled. To true coaster fans, the demolition of these two great rides was unforgivable. It was an act of sabotage. There were outpourings of anger mixed with sadness. An obituary appeared in coaster magazine *Inside Track* shortly afterward:

▲ Mr Twister, at Elitch Gardens, regarded as the greatest spiral-track wooden coaster ever built.

"Earlier this past summer, when I heard the news of the finalization of Elitch Gardens move to a new site, I immediately made plans to visit the old park one last time, to say goodbye to a fine traditional establishment, and especially to get some final rides on two classic woodies, the Wildcat and Mr. Twister. The Twister, they said, was being moved but it was going to be remodeled—that was as good as scrapping it in my opinion! The Wildcat was not going to be moved. That was a grave error in my opinion. Let me say something about Mr. Twister. Twister has always been a favorite of mine and in my opinion it was John Allen's masterpiece. After riding it again my opinion is confirmed and reinforced as I now feel that Twister was one of the all-time greats, ranking with the very best I had ridden ... and I had ridden the Riverside Cyclone, the original Texas Cyclone, and the original Coney Island Cyclone. So you may ask, if Twister was really that outstanding, why are they tampering with near perfection? Would you contemplate painting over the Mona Lisa to try to improve it, that's just what Elitch are doing to John Allen's masterpiece!"

Clearly the new Elitch Gardens was not looking to coaster fans alone to swell their gates to two million by the turn of the century. They have taken long-term projections on the demographic split of the population and come to realize that there are going to be many more fifty year-olds (27 percent) and wealthy pensioners (14 percent) by the year 2010, assuming the same birth rate, than any other age group. If they are going to be successful long term, then they must provide high-quality entertainment and "soft

◄ Twister II, the remodeled Mr. Twister at the new Elitch Gardens, may look pretty fearsome, but it's a pale shadow of its predecessor as a ride.

▲ The structure of Twister II just can't be beaten for its sheer good looks.

rides"—simulated experiences and virtual reality—targeted at this group, as well as wholesome family entertainment, kids' play areas, games of skill, good food, live shows, water gardens, and plush lawns. Simulated rides do not impose the same physical punishment or the bruised ribs and the loss of wallets, as gravity rides like roller coasters. That's why they are keeping only one roller coaster, rebuilding it to look even more striking than the original, and naming it Twister II. For looks alone it must be the fairy castle of all wooden coaster structures, looking just like a giant, white frosted wedding cake a 100 feet high. But is it the last of its kind?

Has the gamble paid off to date? Elitch lashed out $100 million to move site. $58 million went on the hard construction of buildings, pavilions, roadways, pathways, new infrastructure, landscape, and planting. A further $18 million went on rides and attraction—there are twenty-eight in all. $7 million went on land purchase, $7 million on working capital, and $4 million went on legal and finance fees, leaving $6 million for reserves and contingency. The park has been open for two years and is expected to be in the black in two years time, assuming that patrons come to Elitch Gardens in the numbers that they are forecasting.

PARAMOUNT'S KINGS ISLAND

April 29, 1972, is the day that the second golden age of the roller coaster began. It was on this day that Kings Island, Cincinnati, opened John Allen's blinding white wonder, the Racer. Allen had a thing about white, symmetrical structures and precision in detail. Two faster and better roller coasters were already up and running by the time the Racer opened. There was the Thunderbolt at Kennywood, which was the refurbished 1926 Pippin of John Miller, and another of John Allen's masterpieces, Mr. Twister at Elitch Gardens. The Racer was fast but not terrifying and did not scare families away. It also proved to be fun for both coaster buffs and first-time riders. In recent years the popularity and fame of the Racer has been overshadowed by the rampaging Beast and the knotted inversions of Vortex, now occupying center stage at Kings Island.

Let's relive a moment of history through the Racer and ponder the future for the classic roller coaster at Kings Island. The Racer made the biggest impact of any coaster of its day because it simply was the most beautiful, photogenic coaster ever seen. Kings Island had wisely built up the reputation of a park that salvaged and cared about old rides, even devoting a section of park to the memory of Coney Island, Cincinnati. And the Racer was a blast from the past, a combination of modern technology fused onto a 30s' racing coaster, only bigger. It was brightly painted, it had a smooth, rapier-straight

▲ The awesome Beast sets off down the first drop to cut a swathe through the treetops at Kings Island.

▼ The gorgeous symmetry of the lacewing layout of John Allen's Racer at Paramount's Kings Island.

▲ The giant lift hill of The Beast, the longest wooden coaster in the world.

out and back layout, ending with a split track at one end, that sent each coaster on its own fan curve before doubling back along itself. Allen admitted to being inspired by the La Montana Rusa, built by National Amusement Devices in Mexico City. It was also the first wooden coaster to be built in a modern-day theme park.

The Racer was used on many TV commercials, starred in the film *Roller Coaster* and generally rekindled the love affair with the public, who in the 60s had turned away from amusement parks. Gate receipts doubled in a short space of time, Kings Island prospered and invested in more thrill rides in the succeeding years—rides like the giant wooden Beast, the six inversion Vortex, the stand-up King Cobra, the runaway train Adventure Express, and Top Gun.

The Racer is still there but it's looking careworn with its paint peeling. Will Kings Island remain a premier roller coaster haven in the future? More importantly, will the roller coaster be the king of the attractions in the future as far as Kings Island is concerned? Or is the blistered paint work of the Racer a sign of things to come? Here's what Al Weber, chief of operations of Paramount, had to say when he was interviewed by the author in September 1997.

Bennett Tell us a little about the concept of your Days of Thunder motion theaters.

Weber We felt that if we were going to build something around one of these movie

◀ The Racer, surely the most photogenic coaster ever built in its time. The trains race each other along the out-and-back track, but the blue train on the left runs backward. You have been warned!

themes that there would have to be an authenticity that puts you right in the movie environment. When we called it Days of Thunder, it had to be identified with that movie in every detail. So we used the actual movie footage and transferred it into the special effect—the Ubbi Iwerks system—where the seats you sit on, bank, dip, and track the moving 3D image on the screen. We are so pleased with the results that we have it now in all our parks.

Bennett Where does the roller coaster fit into the scheme of things? Do you see a change in direction for a great roller coaster park like Kings Island?

Weber The shift in emphasis to more movie theater experience does not mean that we will phase out or diminish the roller coaster or the white knuckle experience. On the contrary, our cinematic experiences will be more thrill ride oriented than movie theater experience, with the roller coaster tracking say a segment of a disaster movie or being a racing car doing the Indy 100. For example, our Outer Limits ride, which we have built at all our parks and has been a tremendous success. It is essentially an enclosed roller coaster ride with 3,000 feet of track which features four loops, lots of spiral dips, and is built inside a large airplane hangar structure. We use the roller coaster to simulate a journey into outer space and "first contact" with an alien world, with lots of special lighting, and sound effects. And roller coasters are the icons of our parks, particularly at Kings

▲ The enclosed Outer Limits roller coaster ride at Kings Island features loops, spirals, and dips, all taking place in the dark.

◄ The stand-up steel coaster King Cobra, diving down a vertical loop, surely gives the nearest sensation to throwing yourself off a cliff!

▲ Mainstreet, Disneyland, California. © Disney.

Island, so we cannot afford to neglect our traditional base and core market of providing exceptional white knuckle rides.

Bennett There is a demographic shift in the age group towards the over forty-fives. Do you think in building such thrill rides linked with cinematic experiences you might turn away the very young and the older age groups?

Weber We are seeing a wide age range coming to our park to enjoy these rides, from seven year-olds to the over forty-fives, kids coming with their grandparents, as well as unaccompanied teenagers and adults of both sexes. Cinematic theater linked with a white knuckle ride certainly appeals to both the sexes, because it offers romance and fantasy in the mix as well as the thrill ride. And we are getting a whole lot of repeat visits. You must remember that 80 percent of gate receipts come from repeat visits to the park and only 20 percent from new customers each year. In the second year after the Outer Limits ride opened, the line-ups are just as long, so it's very gratifying.

Since the Outer Limits ride was launched at Kings Island, attendances have gone up from 3.2 to 3.5 million visitors a year, each paying $30.95 for the one-price entry. Paramount are also considering the Star Trek Experience to add to the recent Nickleodeon World they introduced for seven to twelve year-olds, with merchandizing, slapstick events, custard pie throwing, face painting, children's shows, and a nostalgic wooden roller coaster ride.

THE DISNEY DIMENSIONS

No other park or individual has had a greater impact on leisure and tourism in the past fifty years than Disneyland Theme Parks and Walter Elias Disney. Today, Disney Enterprises is the largest amusement park and holiday conglomerate in the world. In the U.S. in 1995 it attracted over forty-five million visitors to centers at Disneyland in California, and Walt Disney World incorporating Magic Kingdom, EPCOT, and the Disney-MGM Studios in Florida.

Disney have also broadened their operating base overseas and established major theme parks in Japan and France. Tokyo Disneyland in Japan attracted sixteen million visitors in 1995, the most for any park in the world, while Disneyland in Paris

▲ Mickey and Minnie Mouse at Disneyland, Paris.
© Disney.

had nearly eleven million. Disney theme parks occupy the top six places in the top ten most visited theme parks in the world. Their competitors have tried to mimic and develop the Disney formula into their parks. But none of them can match the success in gate receipts and attendance that Disney have consistently achieved over the years.

Disneyland was not the first theme park concept; many would argue that it was started on Coney Island in the 1900s. It was a modern revival, a renaissance in the tradition of the Steeplechase and Luna Parks, but without the sensorial overload, the titillation of

▲ The entrance to Space Mountain at Disneyland, Paris. © Disney.

freak shows, and emphasis on boy-meets-girl scenario. Walt Disney linked the image of the park with the Mickey Mouse cartoon shows and characters that appeared on his weekly television shows—a powerful marketing and advertising vehicle for the new park.

Disneyland was a three-dimensional extension of that cartoon world, where no one really got hurt, where there was laughter and excitement without pain, and a happy ending to every story. It was a place where you could meet Davy Crockett and beat the Mexicans in Frontier Land, confront the technology of the future in Tomorrow Land, and relive the myth of fairy tales in Fantasy Land. The buildings were faithfully reproduced, albeit in glass fiber and timber; scenic backdrops were made to full scale. Main Street, at the entrance to the park, was built with a Civic Hall, emporium, train station, barber shop, and saloon bar, very reminiscent of American culture of the past, where middle-class values were upheld, where there was no poverty, nor reminders of pluralism—everything was in apple-pie order.

Moreover the classic roller coaster layout was not central to Walt Disney's plans. Gravity rides were developed with Arrow Dynamics, to help create the novel experiences and visual events that were dreamed up by the small team of Disney "imagineers." The ride was a means of conveying people through the experience—the ride was not the experience. That's where the Disney differed from the conventional gravity ride. To coaster buffs

Disney's finest contribution to the roller coaster evolution was the Matterhorn, which introduced the first steel running track with cars riding on nylon wheels. It was an entirely new structure for roller coasters and a new ride experience, and the first steel roller coaster to be built. The car's silent wheels made plummeting through the enclosed spaces of the ride a less ear-shattering experience.

When Walt Disney World opened in Florida in 1970, it was compared to New York's Rockefeller Center for its vast "metropolis" masterplan. Architects and town planners from all over the world came to study its layout, its traffic-efficient designs and traffic patterns. It was the largest amusement park ever built, covering an area of forty-three square miles with many residential resort villages, a camper village, a Magic Kingdom, hotels, golf courses, lakes, water parks, and conference centers.

The Magic Kingdom did have dark thrills rides within its vast enclosure for the first time, although Walt Disney never really wanted them. This was a gesture by Disney, in acknowledging the popularity of thrill rides in theme parks around the U.S. This concept was repeated successfully in Disneyland, Paris, and is one concept that Disney may continue to develop for the future. Space Mountain took ten years from drawing board to completion, and was a huge investment at $36 million, costing as much as the combined cost of the whole of the first Disneyland in Anaheim, California.

▲ A close-up of the "cannon," through which the coaster cars are hauled up to the top of the Space Mountain to begin this dark ride. © Disney.

▲ An atmospheric shot of Space Mountain at sunset over California. © Disney.

▲ The spiraling steel track within Space Mountain is themed with lights and dramatic music, to simulate a flight into space. © Disney.

No other park has successfully innovated the dark ride experience quite like Disney. But there is a snobbery among coaster buffs, that such rides are not macho enough either because they are not fast nor, by the nature of the layout, an outright white knuckle ride. That's a lot of nonsense. If you can be exhilarated and convinced that you are aboard a flight to Saturn while riding a roller coaster, does it matter that your ribs are not hurting at the end of the journey, when you got back to planet Earth? It's the gravity ride that gives that physical sensation, with the illusion of speed created by riding in total darkness.

When Allen Ambrosini interviewed Tony Baxter, the chief guru of Disney's Imagineers for *At The Park* magazine, it was to find out if Disney were going to phase out the roller coaster, as their parks are overhauled and rebuilt in the future.

"The simulator is not going to be the end of roller coasters and all the things that people predicted. We have a couple of things that are really the zenith. Space Mountain in Disneyland, Paris, is one. I think it will be the leader in pushing catapult launches onto coasters around the world. The mountain idea had a lot of things that were a first. Not only did we have the first catapult launch, but the musical score on board [the ride] is phenomenal. The poor guy who composed the score had to ride it continuously in order to orchestrate all the different movements. As we have inversions in the dark, so the combination of dramatic lighting and music adds up to a really extraordinary ride. Disney tries to make family attractions, at the same time pushing the limits on making a ride wild but not physically fast. What's great about the music … is it works like a narrator. In *Jaws*, where the shark was about to attack the swimming girl, John William's score prepared you for the moment leading up to it. On Space Mountain the same thing happens. That gives it a very unique characteristic. On most rides you rely on your eyes clueing you in on what's next, but on this ride it is more of a cinematic experience."

Disney are world market leaders in the leisure industry. They know their customers and know how to present their products well. What Disney do today, the rest will be sure to copy tomorrow.

JAPAN AND THE FAR EAST

One big problem with Japan and the Far East is that travel and accommodation can be expensive, and information on parks almost nonexistent, making planning your itinerary rather hard. Clearly Japan is the premier roller coaster country in the Far East, followed by Korea. Tokyo Disneyland attracts nearly sixteen million visitors, Toshimean Amusement Park in Tokyo and Lotte World in Seoul, South Korea, attract around six million, with Seoul Land, based on the Disneyland concept, attracting over three million. As you travel this part of the world in search of thrill rides, useful tips on the best way to get around in a country are worth knowing. In Japan a rail pass is best, though it could be quite expensive. In South Korea it's the buses which run to schedule, and in the Philippines it's the bus or the jeepnee. Car rental is not recommended except in Australia and New Zealand. A good guidebook for travel is an essential purchase.

Japan has a vast number of amusement parks and roller coasters, mainly steel ones because of the seismic and earthquake regulations, and is second only to the U.S. in the number of parks. With the help of some firsthand accounts from Andrew Lea and John and June Caudwell that appeared in *First Drop* magazine, here is a flavor of what you can expect in the Far East.

In Korea the biggest indoor amusement park in Asia is Lotte World in Seoul. Although it's not as big as West Edmonton Mall in Canada, it is more impressive because it is on such a grand scale. It is built above a huge department store with some of the rides under cover and some built in the parking lot adjacent to the enclosure. There are good visual backdrops to the rides, a vast three-story log flume, a looping coaster by Vekoma called the Orient Express, and a really good ride, the Comet. It is a nice place to visit and is recommended if you are in Seoul. The smaller version of Lotte World is Lotte World Sky Place in Pusan City in the south. It has the only spiral coaster in the world based on the pipeline

▲ Itamin's heartline spinning Spiral Coaster at Sky Plaza, Lotte World, Pusan, South Korea.

▲ The tallest steel coaster in the world is aptly named Fujiyama, with the real Mt. Fujiyama in the background, and is in Fujikyu Highlands Park, Japan.

coaster prototype, that was first developed by Arrow.

One of the most popular parks in Japan is Kijima Park located in Beppu. It is an amusement park in a garden setting.

"Here there are landscaped gardens with lots of topiary—quite unusual for coaster parks in Japan—with bushes and hedges trimmed into animal shapes and odd signs for 'bug houses' dotted all over the place. On investigation you will find it is a place where children can play with live insects of various shapes and sizes. Yuk! The food is good but not cheap and we were supplied maps of the park which is unusual in Japan," remarks John Caudwell. "The Hello Gate as you enter the park can be amusing on hearing a Japanese version of an English welcome."

What Kijima park also has is the best wooden coaster ride in Japan and the only wooden coaster designed by Curtis Summers for Intamin in the Far East—the Jupiter.

"It looks absolutely incredible set against the green hills in the background and the second drop gave us the best thrill of any ride we have ridden. There is a beer house right next to the ride exit which was very welcome."

Fujikyu Highlands Park, located not far from Gotemba city, is a popular theme park in Japan, because of its two white knuckle rides, Moonsault Scramble and the fabulous Fujiyama, the tallest steel coaster in the world. Fujikyu is situated on a hillside with the spectacular views of Mount Fujiyama in the background. Whilst that sounds great, it must be remembered Mount Fujiyama is usually covered in cloud in the cooler months. Fujikyu opens at 9 a.m. and there can be a line-up even if you arrive at 8.30 in the morning.

Tickets to theme parks in Japan are the same everywhere; you can either buy tickets per ride or get a day pass. Cost for white knuckle ride tickets are 1,000 Yen ($8) per ride, and a day pass may set you back 3,500 Yen ($28). Due to frost on the tracks on the day Andrew Lea visited the park, he had to wait two hours before Fujiyama opened. He also went on the feared Moonsault Scramble, which sat starkly on a black pancake of asphalt, but as a ride he rated it as intense as Schwarzkopf's wonderful Mindbender at West Edmonton Mall in Canada. According to Lea, there is only one other ride worth trying at Fujikyu, a double looping coaster, but for the novelty of experiencing a horrible kiddie coaster he would recommend the Fighting Coaster.

Lovers of Blackpool Pleasure Beach and Astroland Park, built on a hardstanding of asphalt and concrete, will find Luna Park in Melbourne, Australia, a nostalgic trip back in time. This is where one of the oldest roller coasters in the world, the Scenic Railway built in 1912, still operates. Luna Park is located in St. Kilda's, a ten-minute drive out of Melbourne, or you can take an old-style electric tram ride from Swanston Street. The tram drops you opposite the laughing face and twin towered entrance to Luna Park, a pastiche of the famous Luna Park of Coney Island. A brake man controls the speed of the train standing in the middle of the ten-car ride. Luna Park in Melbourne is a gem of a place, a wonderful old-style amusement park which has been carefully restored. There are other attractions, including a Coney Island-type Fun House, a beautiful PTC carousel with original hand-carved horses, a steel Big Dipper by Arrow, and a Wild Mouse ride.

If you can make it, then Australia is worth a visit because, besides two old-world Luna Parks in Melbourne and Sydney, there is a fantastic scenic coaster ride in Katoomba Park high up in the Blue Mountains north of Sydney. Modern white knuckle rides abound with good looping coasters built by Intamin and Vekoma in Australia's Wonderland in Sydney, and the theatrically themed Movieworld and Dreamworld along the glorious Gold Coast.

◄ For many coaster fans who have ridden the Bandit at Yomiuri Land, Japan, this is the most intense nonlooping ride in the Far East.

And Finally Some Statistics

Most parks do not want to divulge figures on annual receipts and turnover, but they are quite happy to see their parks high on the top ten list of most visited parks in the world, if they are published.

With the help of IAAPA and NAPHA and *Amusement Business*, it is interesting to see the attendance figures and changes in the pecking order over the years. It may be an estimate but the rankings are comparatively true.

▲ Kumba at night, Busch Gardens, Tampa, Florida.

In the U.S. in 1989, this was the ranking by visiting numbers in millions (ref *Amusement Business*):

1	Walt Disney World Resort, Florida (Magic Kingdom and EPCOT)	30.0
2	Disneyland Park, Anaheim	14.4
3	Universal Studios, Hollywood	5.1
4	Knott's Berry Farm	5.0
5	Sea World, Florida	3.9
6	Sea World, California	3.8
7	Busch Gardens, Tampa	3.5
8	Kings Island, Ohio	3.2
9	Cedar Point, Sandusky	3.2
10	Six Flags Magic Mountain, Valencia, California	3.1

This was the ranking for the rest of the world in 1989 (ref *Amusement Business*):

1	Tokyo Disneyland	12.0
2	Jaya Ancol Dreamland, Jakarta, Indonesia	10.0
3	Blackpool Pleasure Beach, England	6.5
4	Tivoli Gardens, Copenhagen	4.5
5	Riyadh Amusement Park, Saudi Arabia	3.0
6	Toshimaen Amusement Park, Tokyo	3.0
7	Liseberg, Gothenburg, Sweden	2.8
8	Tivoli Gardens, Rio De Janeiro	2.5
9	Alton Towers, Staffordshire, England	2.4
10	Efteling, Kattsheuvel, Holland	2.3

In 1995 IAAPA published the following figures for park attendance around the world. This is their ranking list in millions:

1	Disneyland, Tokyo	15.5
2	Disneyland, California	14.1
3	Magic Kingdom, Florida	12.9
4	Disneyland, Paris	10.7
5	EPCOT, Disney, Florida	10.7
6	Disney MGM Studios, Orlando, Florida	9.5
7	Universal Studios, Florida	8.0
8	Blackpool Pleasure Beach, England	7.5
9	Yong In Farmland, South Korea	7.3
10	Hakkelima Sea Paradise, Japan	6.0

It's pretty obvious that Jaya Ancol Dreamland in Jakarta, the biggest city in the southern hemisphere, must have closed, otherwise they would surely be contending for third spot with the Magic Kingdom. But, whatever the rankings, it's very evident that there are a lot more people visiting Disney theme parks than any other in the world. Some parks, like Blackpool Pleasure Beach, for example, have free entry and a pay per ride policy, making the rankings by statistics look deceptive when comparing turnover against a park like Alton Towers which has 2.5 million visitors, and a one-price entry and free ride policy. Most parks in the U.S. have a one-price entry and free ride policy.

In 1996 Busch Gardens, Tampa, had a record year for attendance, with gates up by 10 percent on the previous year, thanks to two new roller coaster rides, Montu and Kumba. While in gloomy contrast Elitch Gardens, who had moved location in 1994 and had not built any new rides in 1996, had a drop of 10 percent on the previous year's attendance figures. No new attractions means no new customers.

According to Tim O'Brien, the journalist who compiles the estimates of annual park attendance for *Amusement Business*, parks that have added larger roller coaster rides in recent years have been successful in jumping their gate attendance by at least 7–10 percent. "Coasters are sexy additions to the park and usually garner great attention from the local as well as the national media." A really good coaster can put a small pleasure park on to the international map almost overnight. "Take Holiday World, Santa Claus, Indiana," he goes on to explain, "it was just a small family park catering for children's rides until the wooden coaster 'The Raven' was built. The Raven was a hit, a great ride, and now coaster buffs and patrons all over the world know about Holiday World."

It's a fact that money builds a successful park, but it must be spent on what patrons want. "New coasters are great, but they must be coupled with massive renovation, upgrading and improvements to the park amenities to help grow park attendance," says O'Brien. That's why park chains, notably Premier in recent times, can buy under-achieving, under-financed parks like Elitch Gardens, sink big bucks into it and bring it back to profitability. "Premier sunk $25 million in Elitch Gardens in 1997. Included in the investment was a new steel coaster, ground improvements, a 10-acre waterpark and a new park image," adds O'Brien. Attendance has grown 67 percent to 1.5 million in the past year.

So what about the future for the roller coaster, those ephemeral webs of tangled wood and steel, and the jewels of the park? They will surely dazzle and catch the eye of the park-going public for another century. Each passing era will crystallize new coaster prototypes that will elbow the older ones into oblivion with the exception of the classic rides, helped by the blade of the bulldozer, and the craze for even greater moments of insane exhilaration. Happy coastering!

▲ Poster for the Raging Wolf Bobs at Geuga Lake. Merchandizing of rides, with T-shirts, badges, and posters is an integral part of amusement park revenue.

GAZETTEER

A Selection of Major Roller Coasters Parks and Rides Around the World

This directory provides information on the major roller coaster rides in amusement parks in the USA, Canada, Mexico, Europe, Japan, South Korea and Australia. The directory is divided by country, then alphabetically by the states or provinces in that country, and then by the name of the amusement park.

The directory is not a comprehensive listing of every roller coaster ride in the world.

▲ A wooden twin-track racing coaster, Thunder Road, at Paramount's Carowinds.

◄ The Manhattan Express in Las Vegas, against a scaled-down mock-up of the New York skyline, which forms the hotel complex. A fine example of a looping steel coaster.

Key to ride symbols

color code: bobsled = red   steel = blue   wood = green

➤ bobsled   ✪ dark ride   ❊ free fall   ❏ junior steel

◯ junior wood   ◆ looping   ❖ mine train   ▥ non looping

↔ shuttle   ▲ stand up   ▼ suspended   ● wood

Bobsled: a trackless coaster whose wheeled cars roll along a trough made of wood or steel, like a real bobsled run.

Steel: a coaster whose running track is made of rigid tubular steel.

Wood: a coaster whose running track is a flat metal plate pinned to a laminated timber rail.

Dark Ride: an enclosed steel coaster ride in the dark, which features lighting and special effects, and where music is often themed with the ride.

Free Fall: a steel track coaster that is either accelerated or lifted up a vertical tower and then allowed to free fall down by gravity.

Junior Steel: a steel coaster with a lift hill under 41 feet.

Junior Wood: a wood coaster whose lift hill is no higher than 41 feet.

Looping: a steel coaster with a track layout that has loops or inversions, where passengers sit upright in the cars.

Mine Train: a steel coaster with box like cars, designed to recreate the sensation of a runaway mine train and features lots of sharp turns, short dips and tunnel sections.

Non Looping: a steel coaster with a track layout that has no loops, where passengers sit upright in the cars.

Shuttle: a steel coaster that travels or shuttles back and forth on the same length of track and has loop element(s) in the middle section.

Stand Up: a steel coaster with a track layout that usually has loops or inversions, where passengers stand upright in the coaster car.

Suspended: a steel coaster with a track layout that usually has loops or inversions, where passengers sit suspended below the track, like riding a ski lift chair. A few do not loop because they have gondolas that swing.

UNITED STATES

California

1 Belmont Park, San Diego—● Giant Dipper

2 Disneyland, Anaheim—✪ Space Mountain, ✤ Big Thunder, ➤ Matterhorn Bobsleds

3 Great America, Santa Clara—● Blue Streak, ◆ Demon, ■ Grizzly, ↔ Tidal Wave,
▲ Vortex, ▼ Invertigo

4 Knott's Berry Farm, Buena Park—↔ Montezooma's Revenge, ↔ Boomerang,
◆ Wind Jammer

5 Santa Cruz Beach, Santa Cruz—● Giant Dipper, ■ Jet Star

6 Six Flags Magic Mountain, Valencia—● Colossus, ✤ Gold Rusher, ▼ Ninja,
● Psyclone, ◆ Revolution, ◆ Viper, ▼ Batman The Ride, ✳ Superman The Escape,
▲ Riddlers Revenge

▲ A bobsled ride.

Colorado

7 Elitch Gardens, Denver—● Twister II

Florida

8 Busch Gardens, Tampa—◆ Python, ◆ Scorpion, ▼ Montu, ◆ Kumba

9 Walt Disney World, Orlando—✤ Big Thunder Mountain, ✪ Space Mountain

Georgia

10 Six Flags Over Georgia, Atlanta—✪ Mine Train, ● Georgia Cyclone,
● Great American Scream Machine, ◆ Mind Bender, ✳ Z Force,
▼ Batman The Ride

▲ A junior wooden coaster, Scooby Doo, at Paramount's Carowinds.

◀ A wooden out-and-back coaster, the Hoosier Hurricane, at Indiana Beach, Monticello.

Indiana

11 Indiana Beach, Monticello—● Hoosier Hurricane

12 Holiday World, Santa Claus—● Raven

Iowa

13 Adventureland, Des Moines—◆ Dragon, ● Tornado

Illinois

14 Six Flags Great America, Gurnee—● American Eagle, ◆ Demon, ▲ Iron Wolf,
➤ Rolling Thunder, ◆ Shock Wave, ▼ Batman The Ride

Key to ride symbols

color code:	bobsled = red	steel = blue	wood = green	➤ bobsled	✪ dark ride	✳ free fall	❑ junior steel
◯ junior wood	◆ looping	✤ mine train	■ non looping	↔ shuttle	▲ stand up	▼ suspended	● wood

Kansas

15 Joyland Amusement Park, Wichita—● Roller Coaster

Kentucky

16 Kentucky Kingdom, Louisville—■ Starchaser, ● Thunder Run, ▲ Chang

Maryland

17 Adventure World, Largo—● Wilde One

Massachusetts

18 Riverside Park, Agawan—● Riverside Cyclone, ● Thunderbolt, ▼ Mind Eraser

19 Whalom Park, Lunenburg—● Comet Flyer

Michigan

20 Michigan's Adventure, Muskegon—● Wolverine Wildcat, ● Shivering Timbers

Minnesota

21 Valleyfair, Shakopee—■ Wild Thing, ■ Excalibur, ● High Roller, ◆ Corkscrew

Missouri

22 Six Flags Mid-America, Eureka—◆ Ninja, ↔ Mr Freeze, ● Screamin' Eagle

23 Worlds Of Fun, Kansas City—◆ Orient Express, ● Timber Wolf, ■ Mamba

Nevada

24 Buffalo Bill's Resort Casino, Primm—■ Desperado

25 Grand Slam Canyon, Las Vegas—◆ Canyon Blaster

New Jersey

26 Clementon Park, Clementon—● Jack Rabbit

27 Six Flags Great Adventure—◆ Great American Scream Machine, ↔ Lightning
    Loops, ● Rolling Thunder, ◆ Shockwave, ◆ Viper, ↔ Batman & Robin, The Chiller

28 Morey's Pier, North Wildwood—▼ Great Nor'Easter

New York

29 Coney Island's Astroland—● Cyclone

30 Darien Lake, Theme Park—● Predator, ◆ Viper, ↔ Boomerang

▲ Looping steel coaster, Dragon, situated at Adventure Land.

▼ A mine train, The Gold Rush, at Paramount's Carowinds.

◀ Corkscrew steel coaster at Knotts Berry Farm.

Key to ride symbols

color code:	bobsled = red	steel = blue	wood = green	➤ bobsled	✪ dark ride	✳ free fall	❏ junior steel
○ junior wood	◆ looping	❖ mine train	■ non looping	↔ shuttle	▲ stand up	▼ suspended	● wood

▲ A free fall coaster, Demon Drop, at Cedar Point.

31 Playland Park, Rye—● Dragon Coaster, ◆ Whirlwind, ○ Kiddy Coaster

32 The Great Escape, Lake George—● Comet

North Carolina

33 Paramounts Carowinds, Charlotte—◆ Carolina Cyclone, ❖ Gold Rush, ○ Scooby Doo, ● Thunder Road, ● Hurler, ▲ Vortex

Ohio

34 Americana Amusement Park, Middletown—● Screechin' Eagle

35 Cedar Point, Sandusky—▲ Mantis, ▼ Raptor, ▦ Magnum XL-200, ● Mean Streak, ▦ Gemini, ● Blue Streak, ▼ Iron Dragon, ❖ Mine Train, ◆ Corkscrew, ❑ Jnr Gemini, ✳ Demon Drop, ➢ Disaster Transport

36 Geauga Lake, Aurora—● Big Dipper, ◆ Corkscrew, ▼ Serial Thriller, ● Raging Wolf Bobs

37 Paramount Kings Island, Kings Island—● Beast, ● Racer, ▲ King Cobra, ◆ Vortex, ➢ Adventure Express, ○ Beastie, ▼ Top Gun, ✪ Outer Limits, ❖ Mine Train

Oklahoma

38 Frontier City, Oklahoma City—◆ Silver Bullet, ● Wildcat

Pennsylvania

39 Conneaut Lake Park, Conneaut Lake—● Blue Streak

40 Dorney Park, Allentown—▦ Steel Force, ● Hercules, ◆ Lazer, ● Thunderhawk

41 Hershey Park, Hershey—● Wildcat, ● Comet, ↔ Sidewinder, ◆ Sooperdooperlooper, ❖ Trailblazer, ▼ The Great Bear

42 Kennywood Park, West Mifflin—● Jack Rabbit, ● Racer, ◆ Steel Phantom, ● Thunderbolt

43 Knoebels Amusement Resort, Elysburg—● Phoenix, ▦ Jet Star

44 Lakemont Park, Altoona—● Leap The Dips

▲ A looping coaster, Vortex, at Paramount's Carowinds.

Tennessee

45 Libertyland, Memphis—◆ Revolution, ● Zippin Pippin

46 Dollywood, Pigeon Forge—❖ Thunder Express

Texas

47 Astroworld, Houston—▦ Excalibur, ↔ Greezed Lightning, ❑ Serpent, ● Texas Cyclone, ▦ Ultra Twister, ▼ XLR-8, ◆ Taz's Texas Tornado

48 Six Flags Over Texas—↔ Flashback, ● Judge Roy Dream, ● Texas Giant, ◆ Shock Wave, ❖ Mine Train, ❑ Mini Mine Train, ➢ Avalanche, ↔ Mr. Freeze

49 Fiesta Texas, San Antonio—● Rattler, ❖ Roadrunner Express

Utah

50 Lagoon & Pioneer Village, Farmington—◆ Colossal Fire Dragon, ▦ Jet Star II, ● Roller Coaster

Virginia

51 Busch Gardens, Williamsburg—▼ Alpengeist, ▼ Big Bad Wolf,

◆ Loch Ness Monster

52 Paramount Kings Dominion, Doswell—◆ Anaconda, ➤ Avalanche, ● Grizzly,

● Rebel Yell, ◯ Scooby Doo, ▲ Shockwave, ▼ Top Gun, ▼ Volcano

West Virginia

53 Camden Park, Huntingdon—● Big Dipper, ◯ Lil' Dipper, ↔ Thunderbolt Express

MEXICO

1 La Feria Chapultec Magico, Mexico City—● Serpent Of Fire (La Montana Rusa)

CANADA

1 Fantasyland, West Edmonton Mall, Alberta—❑ Auto Sled, ◆ Mindbender

2 Playland Amusement Park, Vancouver—■ Super Big Gulp, ● Roller Coaster

3 Canada's Wonderland, Maple, Ontario—◆ Dragon Fyre, ◯ Ghoster Coaster,

● Minebuster, ▼ Vortex, ▲ Skyrider, ● Wilde Beast, ↔ Bat

4 Marineland, Niagara Falls, Ontario—◆ Dragon Mountain

5 La Ronde Amusement Park, Montreal, Quebec—↔ Le Boomerang, ● Le Monstre,

petites ❑ Montagnes Russes, ◆ Le Super Manege, ❑ Le Cobra

▲ Heartline spinning Ultra Twister at Astroworld, Houston.

◀ The Serpent of Fire, formerly La Montana Rusa, at La Feria Chapultepec, Magico, Mexico City.

Key to ride symbols

color code:

bobsled = red	steel = blue	wood = green	➤ bobsled	✪ dark ride	✳ free fall	❑ junior steel
◯ junior wood	◆ looping	❖ mine train	■ non looping	↔ shuttle	▲ stand up	▼ suspended	● wood

▲ A suspended nonlooping coaster, The Vampire, at Chessington World of Adventures, England.

▼ An old-style Scenic Railway roller coaster with brakeman, at Great Yarmouth Pleasure Beach, England.

EUROPE

 **GREAT BRITAIN**

1 Alton Towers, Alton, Staffordshire—▼ Nemesis, ▦ Beast, ✪ Blackhole, ◆ Corkscrew, ❏ Beastie, ❖ Mine Train, ❏ Oblivion

2 Blackpool Pleasure Beach, Blackpool, Lancashire—▥ Pepsi Max Big One, ● Grand National, ● Big Dipper, ↔ Revolution, ● Roller Coaster, ● Wild Mouse, ▦ Steeple Chase, ○ Zipper Dipper, ✪ Space Invader, ➤ Avalanche, ▦ Tokaydo Express

3 Chessington World Of Adventures, Chessington, Surrey—▼ Vampire, ❖ Mine Train, ❏ Clown Around, ❏ Rattlesnake

4 Drayton Manor Park, Tamworth, Staffordshire—▲ Shockwave, ◆ Python, ❏ Mini Dragon

5 Dreamland, Margate, Kent—● Scenic Railway, ❏ Big Apple

6 Flamingoland, Malton, North Yorkshire—↔ Bullet, ◆ Corkscrew, ✪ Thunder Mountain, ◆ Crazy Loop, ❏ Dragon, ❏ Wild Mouse

7 Great Yarmouth Pleasure Beach, Great Yarmouth, Norfolk—● Roller Coaster, ▦ Toboggan

8 Lightwater Valley, Ripon, North Yorkshire—■ Ultimate, ◆ Soopa Looper, ✪ Rat,
  ❑ Ladybird

9 Oakwood, Narbeth, Pembrokeshire—● Megaphobia, ❑ Tree Tops,
  ❑ Kiddie Coaster

10 Pleasureland Amusement Park, Southport, Merseyside—● Cyclone, ❑ Wildcat,
  ❑ Big Apple

11 Rotunda Amusement Park, Folkestone, Kent—● Runaway Coaster, ❑ Juvenile Coaster

12 Thorpe Park, Chertsey, Surrey—❑ Flying Fish

 ## FRANCE

1 Disneyland, Marne la Vallee, Cedex—◆ Temple of Peril, ✤ Big Thunder Mountain,
  ✪ Space Mountain

2 OK Corral, Cuges les Pins, Toulon—■ Katapult

3 Parc Asterix, Plailly, Paris—● Tonnerre de Zeus, ◆ Gouderix, ❑ Vol D'Icare,
  ➤ Trans Averne

4 Walibi Smurf, Metz—● Anaconda, ◆ Comet Space

 ## BELGIUM

1 Bellewaerde, Ieper—↔ Bommerang, ✪ Dark Ride

2 Boobejaanland, Kasterlee—◆ Tornado, ◆ Looping Star, ✪ Revolution, ▼ Air Race

3 Walibi, Wavre—↔ Sirocco, ◆ Tornado, ✤ Colorado

◄ Schwarzkopf Jumbo Jet at Walibi Park, Wavre, Belgium.

Key to ride symbols

| color code: | bobsled = red | steel = blue | wood = green | ➤ bobsled | ✪ dark ride | ✳ free fall | ❑ junior steel |
| ○ junior wood | ◆ looping | ✤ mine train | ■ non looping | ↔ shuttle | ▲ stand up | ▼ suspended | ● wood |

▲ Suspended looping coaster, Invertigo, at Liseberg Gardens, Gothenburg.

▼ The only portable suspended looping coaster in the world, Euro Star.

▲ The fiberglass cars of Thriller, a portable steel looping coaster.

 **HOLLAND**

1 Efteling Family Leisure Park—● Pegasus, ◆ Python

 **DENMARK**

1 Tivoli Gardens, Copenhagen—● Scenic Railway

 **SWEDEN**

1 Liseberg Gardens, Liseberg, Gothenburg—■ Lisebergbanan, ◆ Top Spin, ◆ Galactica, ▼ Invertigo, ❑ Mini Coaster, ↔ Hang Over

 SPAIN

1 Port Aventura, Salou, Costa Dorada—◆ Dragon Khan, ● Stampida, ● Tomahawk, ❖ El Diablo

GERMANY

There are many travelling fairs in Germany, where portable roller coasters are temporarily built on compact sites, and where some of Anton Schwarzkopf's great looping coasters like Thriller and Euro Star are featured.

▲ A twisting wooden track layout for White Canyon at Nagashimi Spaland, Japan.

JAPAN

1 Kijima Park, Beppu—● Jupiter, ▥ Wild Mouse, ❖ Mine Train

2 Fujikyu Highlands, Mt. Fuji—▥ Fujiyama, ↔ Moonsault Scramble

3 Osaka Expoland, Osaka—▼ Orochi, ◆ Space Salamander

4 Yomiuri Land, Tokyo—▥ Bandit, ● White Cyclone

5 Spaceworld, Fukuoka—◆ Titan, ◆ Space Coaster

6 Nagashimi Spaland, Nagoya—● White Cyclone, ◆ Ultra Twister

7 Tokyo Disneyland, Tokyo—✪ Space Mountain, ❖ Thunder Mountain

8 Gotemba Family Land, Gotemba—▼ Gambit, ❖ Mine Train, ▲ Togo Stand Up

9 Mitsui Greenland, Kumamoto—◆ Dinosaur, ▼ Swing Coaster, ◆ Ultra Twister,
   ↔ Shuttle Loop, ▲ Togo Stand Up Racer

10 Hakkejima Sea Paradise, Yokohama—❑ Surf Coaster

11 Himeji Central Park, Himeji—❑ Jet Coaster, ▼ Diavlo

12 Toshimaen, Shinjuku, Tokyo—◆ Top Spin, ◆ Thunder Looper

▼ Togo's unique stand-up racing coasters at Mitsui Greenland, Japan.

SOUTH KOREA

1 Lotte World, Seoul—▥ Comet, ◆ Orient Express

2 Seoul Land, Seoul—◆ Double Loop, ❑ Crazy Mouse, ✪ Blackhole 2000

3 Expoworld, Taejan—◆ Multi Inversion Coaster

4 Lotte World Sky Plaza, Pusan—◆ Spiral Coaster

AUSTRALIA

1 Luna Park, Melbourne—● Scenic Railway, ◆ Dragon Coaster, ◆ Mad Mouse

2 Katoomba Hills, Blue Mountain—▥ Orphan Rocket, ▥ Scenic Railway

3 Australia's Wonderland, Eastern Creek, Sydney—● Bush Beast, ▥ Beastie,
   ↔ Demon, ✳ Space Probe 7

4 Dreamworld, Gold Coast—▥ Thunderbolt, ✳ Tower of Terror

5 Sea World, Gold Coast—◆ Corkscrew, ▥ Thrillseeker

6 Warner Brothers Movie World, Surfers Paradise, Brisbane—▼ Lethal Weapon

▲ Katoomba Hills Scenic Railway, situated in the Blue Mountains of Australia.

Key to ride symbols

| color code: | bobsled = red | steel = blue | wood = green | ➤ bobsled | ✪ dark ride | ✳ free fall | ❑ junior steel |
| ○ junior wood | ◆ looping | ❖ mine train | ■ non looping | ↔ shuttle | ▲ stand up | ▼ suspended | ● wood |

ROLLER COASTER WORLD RECORDS
Compiled by Barry Norman, 1998

The criteria used to establish roller coaster records that appear in the *Guinness Book of Records* are based on the following set of rules:

Tallest Category refers to the lift height as determined from actual engineering drawings and measured from the top of the track at the bottom of the lift, to the top of the track at the lift crown.

Drop (vertical) refers to the vertical distance measured from the top of the track at the lift crown or peak, to the top of the track at the bottom of the following drop or dip.

Length refers to the complete length of the track measured along the center line of the rails.

Complete-circuit Track refers to a continuous circuit track rather than a shuttle (backward and forward) track which repeats track elements during every ride.

Loop/inversion the term "loop" refers to a vertical loop element of a steel track roller coaster. Other types of spirals, such as corkscrew and zero-g-rolls, are termed inversions as opposed to vertical loop elements. It is therefore quite correct to use the terminology "loop/inversion" in describing a multi-inversion coaster.

The 1998 Hall Of Fame

Oldest

The world's oldest operating roller coaster is the Rutschbahnan (Scenic Railway) Mk 2 which was constructed at the Tivoli Gardens, Copenhagen, Denmark, in 1913.

The oldest original operating roller coaster in the U.S. is the Jack Rabbit at Clementon Lake Park, Clementon, New Jersey, built in 1919.

▶ The "Switchback Anno" (1902–1913) at the Tivoli Gardens, Denmark.

The oldest operating roller coaster in England is the Scenic Railway at Dreamland, Margate, which was opened to the public on July 3, 1920.

Longest

The world's longest roller coaster is the Ultimate at Lightwater Valley Park in Ripon, North Yorkshire, England. The tubular steel track measures 1 mile 740 yards in length.

The longest wooden roller coaster in the world is the track of the Beast at Paramount's Kings Island, Ohio, which has a length of 1 mile 706 yards.

Tallest and Fastest

The tallest and fastest roller coaster in the world is Superman The Escape at Six Flags Magic Mountain, Valencia, California. This linear-induction, motor-powered, dual-track, "vertical reverse point" free fall coaster was designed by Intamin of Switzerland and features a 415-foot steel support structure. Each 15-seater passenger car has a design speed of 100 m.p.h.

The tallest complete circuit roller coaster in the world is the steel track of Fujiyama, designed by Togo and located in the Fujikyu Highlands Amusement Park in Japan. It has a chain lift height of 234 feet 7 inches and a first drop of 230 feet.

The tallest complete circuit roller coaster in the U.S. is the steel non-inversion Desperado

▲ Dragon Khan, the coaster with the most inversions and loops (along with Monte Makaya) at Port Aventura, Salyon, Spain.

at Buffalo Bill's Resort Casino, which has a lift height of 209 feet and a first drop of 225 feet—the same as the Steel Phantom at Kennywood Park, the fastest gravity roller in the world with a potential top speed of 80 m.p.h.

The tallest roller coaster in Europe is the steel non-inversion Pepsi Max Big One at Blackpool Pleasure Beach, England, which has a lift height of 201 feet and a first drop of 205 feet.

Most Inversions and Loops

The roller coaster with the most inversions and loops is Dragon Khan at Port Aventura in Spain, designed by Bolliger and Mabillard. Riders are turned upside-down eight times along the steel track which extends 4,166 feet. This record is shared with the "Monte Makaya" in Brazil.

▲ Steel Phantom, the joint fastest (with Desperado) gravity roller coaster in the world.

▶ Fujiyama, the world's tallest complete-circuit roller coaster.

Most Roller Coasters in a Park

Cedar Point in Sandusky, Ohio, with twelve coasters has the most roller coasters operating at an amusement park. The park contains two wood and ten steel track coasters. Blackpool Pleasure Beach, Blackpool, England, is second with eleven operating roller coasters, five wood and six steel track rides.

ROLLER COASTER HISTORY AT A GLANCE

▲ Scenic Railway with traveling brakeman, Coney Island, Brooklyn, New York, 1907.

15th/16th centuries	Russian ice slides, built in St. Petersburg, Russia
1784	First wheeled "coaster carts" used in Russia to extend the riding season
1816	"Russian Mountain" dry slides with wheeled carts are erected in Paris
1843	Tivoli Gardens opens in Copenhagen, Denmark
1848	Wooden Loop the Loop wheeled track ride introduced in Paris, but was not successful
1873	Mauch Chunk gravity railway becomes America's first gravity ride
1884	La Marcus Adna Thompson builds the first true "roller coaster"—the Switchback at Coney Island
1884	Charles Alcoke builds the first continuous-circuit roller coaster at Coney Island
1885	Philip Hinkle builds a roller coaster where the cars are mechanically pulled up the lift hill
1887	Thompson introduces the first Scenic Railway at Atlantic City
1887	First Figure-Eight roller coaster built at Haverhill, Massachusetts
1891	Switchback Railway built at Blackpool, England
1891	Lina Beecher markets the vertical looping Centrifugal Cycle Railway
1895	Paul Boyton's Sea Lion Park opens at Coney Island. Considered to be the first enclosed amusement park, with a gate admission
1897	Steeplechase Park opens at Coney Island
1901	First elliptical vertical-looping ride is built by Edmund Prescott
1903	Luna Park opens at Coney Island
1904	Dreamland opens at Coney Island
1907	Christian Feuchs designs the first high-speed roller coaster, Drop the Dips, and introduces the lap bar to secure riders in their seats
1922	John Miller patents the "uplift" and "guide wheel" safety system for coaster cars
1920s	The first "golden age" of the roller coaster
1930s	The Great Depression in the U.S. causes many parks to close
1952	Cinerama film revives interest in roller coasters
1955	Disneyland opens in Anaheim, Los Angeles, California. The theme park is born
1958	Karl Bacon builds the first steel-track roller coaster, Matterhorn Bobsleds
1964	John Allen builds Mr. Twister, a new maxi wooden coaster ride
1970s	The second "golden age" of the roller coaster
1972	The Racer, a twin-track wooden roller coaster, kick starts a great revival in classic wooden coaster construction
1975	Ron Toomer designs the first Corkscrew coaster
1976	Anton Schwarzkopf designs the first "vertical-loop" steel coaster at Six Flags Magic Mountain
1976	The site and route of the dismantled Mauch Chunk Railway is declared an historical monument
1978	National Amusement Park Historical Association (N.A.P.H.A.) is founded
1979	The Beast, the longest wooden-track roller coaster in the world, is built at Kings Island
1981	Arrow design the first suspended roller coaster for Kings Island
1983	Disneyland opens in Tokyo
1984	Togo build the first "stand-up" coaster at Kings Island
1986	Anton Schwarzkopf designs the multi-inversion Thriller portable roller coaster
1989	Arrow build the first hyper coaster, Magnum XL 200, at Cedar Point. It has the highest lift hill and longest first drop in the world
1991	Cyclone, at Coney Island, becomes an official New York landmark
1992	Bolliger & Mabillard build the first "inverted-swing" suspended roller coaster, Batman The Ride, at Six Flags Great America
1992	The world's longest roller coaster, Ultimate, is built at Lightwater Valley Theme Park, England
1993	Euro Disney, now called Disneyland Paris, opens in France
1994	Desperado, built by Arrow at Buffalo Bill's Resort Casino, becomes the world's tallest roller coaster at 209 feet. It is also the fastest conventional gravity ride at 80 m.p.h. and has the longest first drop of 225 feet—equal to Steel Phantom at Kennywood Park
1995	Dragon Khan, designed by Bolliger & Mabillard at Port Aventura, Salou, Spain, has the most inversions—eight—for a complete circuit roller coaster
1996	Fujiyama, built by Togo at Fujikyu Highlands Park, Japan, becomes the world's tallest roller coaster at 259 feet above ground, and has the highest lift hill of 234 feet 7 inches
1997	Superman The Escape, designed by Intamin AG, opens at Six Flags Magic Mountain, and is the first roller coaster powered by a linear induction motor to launch a coaster car 400 feet up a vertical track at a design speed of 100 m.p.h.
1998	Oblivion, designed by Bolliger & Mabillard at Alton Towers, England, is the first "vertical drop roller coaster"

▲ Oblivion at Alton Towers, England, a new ride concept for 1998.

PICTURE CREDITS

p6 © Busch Entertainment Corp; p8, Photograph: WKVL; p9*t* and *b*, Photograph: WKVL; p10, Photograph: WKVL; p11*t* and *b*, Photograph: WKVL; pp12–13, Mauch Chunk Railway Foundation–Bob Gormley; p12*b*, Mauch Chunk Railway Foundation–Bob Gormley; p14*t*, Photograph: WKVL; p14*b*, Frederick Fried Archives; p15*t*, Photograph: WKVL; p15*m*, Jim Abbate, National Amusement Park Historical Association; p15*b*, Photograph: WKVL; p16*t*, *m* and *b*, Photograph: WKVL; p17, Photograph: WKVL; p18, Photograph: WKVL; p19*t*, Jim Abbate, National Amusement Park Historical Association; p19*b*, Photograph: WKVL; p20*t* and *m*, Jim Abbate, National Amusement Park Historical Association; p20*b*, Photograph: WKVL; p21, Photograph: WKVL; p22*tr*, Kennywood; p22*tl*, Charles J. Jacques Jr. Collection; p22*m*, Kennywood; p22*b*, Cedar Point Historical Archives; p23*t* and *b*, Photograph: WKVL; p24, Photograph: WKVL; p25*t* and *b*, Photograph: WKVL; pp26–7, Charles J. Jacques Jr. Collection; p28, Frederick Fried Archives; p29*t* and *b*, Photograph: WKVL; p30*t*, Kennywood; p30*b* Photograph: WKVL; p31, Photograph: WKVL; p32, Charles J. Jacques Jr. Collection; p33*t* and *b*, Kennywood; p34*t*, IAAPA; p34*m* and *b*, Photograph: WKVL; p35*t* and *b*, Photograph: WKVL; p36*t*, Photograph: WKVL; p36*b*, Tom Maglione; p37*t*, *m* and *b*, Photograph: WKVL; p38*t*, Traver Family Archive; p38*m* and *b*, Photograph: WKVL; p39*t* and *b*, Photograph: WKVL; p40*t* and *b*, Photograph: WKVL; p41*t* and *b*, Photograph: WKVL; p42*m* and *b*, PTC (Philadelphia Toboggan Company; p43*t*, Photograph: WKVL; p43*b*, Tom Maglione; p44, Tom Maglione; pp46–7, Photograph: WKVL; p46*b*, Six Flags Premier Parks.; p47*t*, Paramount Parks Inc.; p47*m*, Six Flags-Premier Parks Inc.; p47*b*, Tom Maglione; p48*t*, Darien Lake; p48*b*, Tom Maglione: p49*t*, Darien Lake; p49*m*, Photograph: WKVL; p49*b*, Denise Dinn-Larick; pp50–1, Cedar Point, Photograph by Dan Feicht; p52*t*, Cedar Point, Photograph by Dan Feicht; p52*b*, Tom Maglione; p53*t*, Paramount Parks Inc.; p53*m*, Darien Lake; p53*b*, © Disney; p54*t*, Blackpool Pleasure Beach; p54*b*, Tom Maglione; p55, Jeffrey Nicholson; p56, Photograph: WKVL; p57, Photograph: WKVL; p58, Photograph: WKVL; p59*t* and *b*, Photograph: WKVL; pp60–1, Photograph: WKVL; p62, Photograph: WKVL; p63*t* and *b*, Photograph: WKVL; p64, Santa Cruz Boardwalk; p67*t*, Six Flags-Premier Parks Inc.; p70*b*, Parc Asterix; p71*t* and *b*, Photograph: WKVL; p72*t*, Photograph: WKVL; p72*m*, Kennywood Park; p72*b*, Intamin; p73, Tom Maglione; p74, Photograph: WKVL; p75*t*, Tom Maglione; p75*m*, Photograph: WKVL; p76*t*, Photograph: WKVL; p76*b*, Dorney Park & Wildwater Kingdom; p77*t* and *b*, Photograph: WKVL; p78*t*, Six Flags-Premier Parks Inc.; p78*b*, Photograph: WKVL; p79, Photograph: WKVL; p80, Tom Maglione; p81, Paramount Parks Inc.; p82, Six Flags-Premier Parks Inc.; p83*t* and *m*, Photograph: WKVL; p84*t* and *b*, Photograph: WKVL; p85, Six Flags-Premier Parks Inc.; p86, Cedar Point, Photograph by Dan Feicht; p87, Photograph: WKVL; p88, Six Flags-Premier Parks Inc.;

p92*t* and *b*, West Edmonton Mall; p93, West Edmonton Mall; p94, Santa Cruz Boardwalk; p95, Santa Cruz Boardwalk; p96, Photograph: WKVL; p97*l* and *r*, Photograph: WKVL; p98*t* and *b*, Alton Towers; p99, Alton Towers; p100*t* and *b*, Tom Maglione; p101*l* and *r*, Tom Maglione; p102, Oakwood; p103, Tom Maglione; p104, Dorney Park and Wildwater Kingdom, Photograph by Dan Feicht; p105, Dorney Park and Wildwater Kingdom; p106, Busch Entertainment Corp; p107, Busch Entertainment Corp; p108, Parc Asterix; p109*t* and *b*, Parc Asterix; p110, Tom Maglione; p111, Tom Maglione; p112*t* and *b*, Wolf Tiemeir, Hills & Thrills Magazine; p113*l* and *r*, Wolf Tiemeir, Hills & Thrills Magazine; p114, Tom Maglione; p115*l*, Holiday World; p115*r*, Tom Maglione; p116, Kennywood; p118*t*, *m*, and *b*, Kennywood; p119*r* and *b*, Kennywood; p120*l*, Kennywood; p120*b* Tom Maglione; p121*t*, Kennywood; p121*b*, Tom Maglione; p122*t* and *b*, Kennywood; p123, Kennywood; p124, Kennywood; p125, Tom Maglione; p126, Tom Maglione; p127, Tom Maglione; pp128–9, Photograph: WKVL; p130*t*, Blackpool Pleasure Beach Archive; p130*b*, Blackpool Pleasure Beach Archive; p131, Lord Lichfield; p132, Blackpool Pleasure Beach; p133*t*, Photograph: WKVL; p133*b*, Tom Maglione; p134*t*, Tom Maglione; p134*b*, Photograph: WKVL; p135*t*, Photograph: WKVL; p135*b*, Blackpool Pleasure Beach; p136*t*, *m*, and *b*, Alton Towers; p137*t*, *m*, and *b*, Alton Towers; p138*t* and *b*, Six Flags-Premier Parks Inc.; p139, Six Flags-Premier Parks Inc.; p141, Six Flags-Premier Parks Inc.; p142, Cedar Point, Photograph by Dan Feicht; p143*t*, Photograph: WKVL; p143*b*, Cedar Point Historical Archives; pp144–5, Cedar Point, Photograph by Dan Feicht; pp146–7, Cedar Point, Photograph by Dan Feicht; p148, Cedar Point; p149, Photograph: WKVL; pp150–1, Cedar Point, Photograph by Dan Feicht; pp152–3, Cedar Point, Photograph by Dan Feicht; p154, Primm Nevada; p155, Tom Maglione; p156, Tom Maglione; p157, Tom Maglione; p158, Tom Maglione; p159*t*, Paramount Parks Inc.; p159*b*, Paramount Parks Inc.; p160, Paramount Parks Inc.; p161*t* and *b*, Photograph: WKVL; p162, Photograph: WKVL; p163, Paramount Parks Inc.; p164, © Disney; p165, © Disney; p166, © Disney; p167*t* and *b*, © Disney; p168, © Disney; p169, Intamin; p170, Togo International; p171; Togo International; p172, Busch Entertainment Corp; p173, Photograph: WKVL; p174, Cashman Photograph; p175, Paramount Parks Inc.; p178, Tom Maglione; p179*t*, Adventure Land; p179*b*, Paramount Carowinds; p180*t*, Intamin; p180*b*, Paramount Carowinds; p181*t* and *b*, Tom Maglione; p182*t*, Chessington World of Adventures; p182*b*, Photograph: WKVL; p183, Photograph: WKVL; p184*t*, Liseberg AB, Stig Kälvelid, Box 5053, 402 22 Göteborg; p184*m* and *b*, Wolf Tiemeir, Hills & Thrills Magazine; p185*t*, Intamin; p185*m*, Togo International; p185*b*, Photograph: WKVL; p186, Photograph: WKVL; p187, Photograph: WKVL; p188*t*, Toussauds Group; p188*b*, Kennywood; p189, Togo International; p190*t*, Photograph: WKVL; p190*b*, George Brooks

USEFUL SOURCES OF INFORMATION

European Coaster Club, c/o *First Drop*, 6 Green Lane, Hillingdon, Middlesex UB8 3EB, England

Mid Atlantic—Coaster Club, 7532 Murillo Street, Springfield, Virginia 22141, USA

National Amusement Park Historical Association (NAPHA), PO Box 83, Mt. Prospect, Illinois 60656, USA

American Coaster Enthusiasts (ACE), PO Box 8226, Chicago, Illinois 60680, USA

WKVL Amusement Research Library, The White House, 41 Linkfield Lane, Redhill, Surrey RH1 1JH, England

USEFUL READING

The Incredible Scream Machine: A History of The Roller Coaster Robert Cartmell, Amusement Park Books, Inc, 1987

Harry G Traver: Legends of Terror Richard Munch, Amusement Park Books, Inc, 1982

Blackpool Pleasure Beach: A Century Of Fun Peter Bennett, Blackpool Pleasure Beach, 1996

White Knuckle Ride Mark Wyatt, Salamander Books Ltd, UK, 1996

Guide To Ride: A Guide To The Roller Coasters of North America an ACE Enterprise Publication, 1991

The American Amusement Park Industry Judith Adams, Twayne Publishers, Boston, USA, 1991

The Amusement Park Guide (North America) Tim O'Brien, The Globe Pequot Press, Connecticut, USA, 1991.

Kennywood: Roller Coaster Capital Of The World Charles Jacques, Jnr, Amusement Park Journal, USA, 1982

Cedar Point: The Queen Of America's Watering Places David and Diana Francis, Daring Books, Ohio, USA, 1988